The
Brownie
Diaries

Leah
Hyslop

For my family, Mum and Dad and Sally and Boo. And in memory of Granny Sophie, who taught me how to bake.

'You would be amazed by what you can give up, lose, or break, and yet still be a person who gets happy over brownies.'
Augusten Burroughs

'This is a great brownie and I'm going to fight you for it.'
Notting Hill

The
Brownie
Diaries

My recipes for happy times, heartbreak and everything in between

Leah Hyslop

BLOOMSBURY ABSOLUTE

LONDON • OXFORD • NEW YORK • NEW DELHI • SYDNEY

BLOOMSBURY ABSOLUTE
Bloomsbury Publishing Plc
50 Bedford Square, London, WC1B 3DP, UK
29 Earlsfort Terrace, Dublin 2, Ireland

BLOOMSBURY, BLOOMSBURY ABSOLUTE,
the Diana logo and the Absolute Press logo
are trademarks of Bloomsbury Publishing Plc

First published in Great Britain 2022

Text © Leah Hyslop, 2022
Photography © Lauren Mclean, 2022

A catalogue record for this book is available
from the British Library.

Library of Congress Cataloguing-in-
Publication data has been applied for.

ISBN: 9781472982780
ePUB: 9781472982773
ePDF: 9781472982766

2 4 6 8 10 9 7 5 3 1

Printed and bound in China by Toppan
Leefung Printing

Bloomsbury Publishing Plc makes every
effort to ensure that the papers used in
the manufacture of our books are natural,
recyclable products made from wood grown
in well-managed forests. Our manufacturing
processes conform to the environmental
regulations of the country of origin.

To find out more about our authors and
books visit www.bloomsbury.com and sign
up for our newsletters.

contents

introduction

whatever your problem in life, a brownie is the solution.

Brownies are irresistible. Densely and damply chocolatey, their fudgy interior barely holding together under a crinkly top, they exert a dark magic that is harder to say no to than a big-eyed puppy or free samples at the supermarket. I only have to glimpse a stack of brownies in a bakery window and I go as gooey as they are.

Like their key ingredient, chocolate, brownies have a near-miraculous ability to make us feel good. A single bite sends sugar and serotonin racing through the body, ready to patch up confidence or piece together a shattered heart. Brownies – and their white chocolate cousins, blondies – make bad days better, and good days even happier. A leaning tower of brownies will bring extra joy to any celebration (though also lots of chocolatey crumbs trodden into your carpet – sorry in advance about that).

Just as there is a brownie for every occasion, there is a brownie for every taste. They can be elegantly simple, without so much as a walnut piercing their dark chocolatey hearts. At the other end of the scale, they can be flavoured with everything from beer to bananas, iced and sprinkled and drizzled and twizzled until they're fancier than Marie Antoinette on a night out. A brownie is a blank canvas for the wildest indulgences of your imagination.

When it comes to texture, the world splits into two camps, Team Fudgy and Team Cakey, and each commands the kind of partisan fervour that civil wars are built on. I've seen my most mild-mannered friends furiously spray brownie out of their mouths as they shout down the opposition. I personally prefer fudgy brownies – that heavy, knock-a-man-out-at-twenty-paces texture is surely what makes them different to any other bake – and most recipes in this book score fairly highly on the squidge-o-meter.* But I do think there is some over-fetishisation of fudginess these days; the type of brownies so rammed with sugar and butter that they dissolve into chocolatey puddles as soon as you step towards them with a knife. There's a time and a place for well-made cakey brownies, too.**

---

* Not an official scoring system.
** The obsession with cakey vs. fudgy also means a very important third category, chewy, is often neglected. This is a bit like how people fixate on John Lennon's musical prowess vs. Paul McCartney's, and completely forget about George and Ringo.

I'm sure part of the reason brownies bring us such joy is how simple they are to make. Just a handful of basic ingredients and a stir of the wooden spoon reliably yields something delicious, something more than the sum of its parts. Yet the perfect brownie – not underbaked, not overbaked – takes a little skill and practice. The exhilaration when you get it right feels like you've just discovered penicillin – but there's no moral obligation to share the results with the rest of the world.

That said, we probably make brownies as much for others as we do for ourselves. A brownie can say a lot of things, very easily and very unfussily. It can say I love you; I might be falling in love with you; I'm sorry; I'm thinking of you; let's be friends; are we still friends? Chocolate has always been linked to love and desire, and to share a brownie is an intimate thing – not least because afterwards you're probably going to have to tell your companion they have chocolate all over their face.

There are people who, when looking back over their lives, can identify occasions and events by the clothes they wore, or the music they listened to. It sounds silly, but I can chart my life in brownies; from the crumbly squares I scoffed in the school canteen, to the everything-but-the-kitchen-sink blondies I inhaled with friends after a break-up. The ritual of baking brownies – melting the chocolate, folding in the flour, scraping leftover batter from the bowl – is as straightforward and soothing to me as popping on a favourite podcast or running a hot bath. Whatever else is going on in the world, a brownie *always* makes things better.

This book is a celebration of the brownie, in all its oozy, gooey, chewy forms. I hope, like any sensible person faced with a tray of homemade brownies, you get stuck straight in.

welcome to brownie school

This section is about the science of making brownies and blondies. Feel free to skip it if you're short on time, want to get cooking straight away or find these long bits at the start of recipe books boring. But if you're a baking nerd, understanding the basic principles of how brownies work might be a help.

Don't tell them this, but at their gooey heart, brownies and blondies are failed cakes. Baked goods are a careful balance of ingredients that give structure (such as flour and eggs) and tenderisers (like fat and sugar), which keep the bake soft. Brownies have a much higher ratio of sugar and butter to flour than, say, a Victoria sponge cake, which stops them rising in the same way; they cook in a sort of collapsed, but delicious, mess.

Let's take a look at the key stages in brownie-making.

stage 1: melt

Most brownie and many blondie recipes begin with melting butter and chocolate. This method is very different to a traditional cake where you start by creaming sugar and butter together, trapping lots of air bubbles to ensure a light and airy result. The melting helps create that uniquely dense texture that makes brownies so good. (When recipes in this book begin with creaming instead, you'll notice the results are much cakier.)

Obviously, chocolate provides that all-important cocoa flavour and 'goo' factor. We all know chocolate contains fat, but it also has particles of protein and starch; these unique qualities can help 'set' baked goods (this is one of the reasons you don't need too much flour in brownies).

Butter – or other fats, such as oil – help make brownies rich and soft, and are crucial for that tender, melt-in-your-mouth texture. This is why, I'm afraid, low-fat brownies often taste like something better suited to sanding down furniture.

Many people melt chocolate and butter in a heatproof bowl, over a saucepan of just-simmering water, which minimises the chances of overheating the chocolate. You're very welcome to adopt this approach if you like to be cautious (or have a tendency to burn things). I, however, prefer to melt the butter and chocolate directly in a saucepan over a low heat, then use the same saucepan as the mixing bowl. You do need to keep a careful eye on the pan, to ensure the ingredients are melting together very gently, but I find this method much easier.

Always break or roughly chop the chocolate into pieces before adding to the pan; chocolate isn't a great conductor of heat, and this encourages it to melt more quickly, without risking the chocolate overheating and splitting.

stage 2: mix

After you've melted the chocolate and butter, it's time to add sugar and eggs. Sugar obviously brings sweetness, but it's also crucial for moisture and texture. The high quantity of sugar in brownies (as well as the Everest-esque mountains of butter and chocolate) is one of the reasons they're so gooey.

Eggs are multi-taskers. They add flavour, richness, moisture and volume, but most importantly, they provide structure. Think of them as the stern headmistress of brownie school, imposing order on the unruly other ingredients. When eggs are agitated by being mixed or heated, the proteins inside unfold then 'bind'

together, giving the bake stability. People often caution against over-beating brownie batter, in the belief that avoiding the introduction of air will ensure the densest, squidgiest results, but you do need to beat your eggs in with some vigour to ensure they disperse well enough to perform all these important jobs. You can tell when you've mixed eggs in properly, as the batter will become thicker, glossier and pull away slightly from the sides of the pan.

Most of my recipes suggest doing all this mixing very gently by hand, to avoid the dreaded over-beating. Occasionally, however, after the introduction of the sugar and eggs, I whizz the batter with a handheld electric whisk, until it's thick and velvety. This seems counterintuitive, but it's actually a neat trick which helps create that coveted papery crust. Essentially, the whisking means a meringue-like layer rises to the top, while the brownies stay soft and gooey below.

stage 3: fold

The last step is to add the flour – plus cocoa, if it's in the recipe, and any other extras, such as fruit or chocolate chips.

Like eggs, flour is crucial for giving brownies and blondies their structure. Flour owes this impressive ability to gluten, a family of proteins that begin to form a network the moment the flour meets liquid. It is this scaffolding structure that holds brownie or blondies together, preventing them from collapsing into a muddy puddle.

You don't need a lot of flour in brownies, but you do need some. Cakey brownie recipes tend to feature a higher quantity of flour, and gooey ones less. Always fold in the flour as gently as you can. Although brownies need gluten, gluten becomes stronger the more you work it, and overmixing can lead to a tough or doughy bake.

stage 4: bake

This is the trickier bit. People have wildly different opinions about brownies; some people want barely-cooked mush, others want squares sturdy enough to tile a kitchen with. And it can be hard to tell, even with your nose squashed against the oven door, exactly how baked a brownie or blondie is.

I've tried to be as helpful as I can, telling you what to look for in each recipe, and giving a range of timings where possible. You will quickly learn to trust your own eyes and know exactly when a brownie is cooked to your liking. It sounds silly, but I can often tell when brownies are ready by the aroma – the second the kitchen begins to smell like chocolate *cake*, as opposed to melted chocolate, I know it's time to pull on my oven gloves.

There are a few tell-tale signs that a brownie is done. If a brownie or blondie is set on top, with a few cracks around the edges, it's probably ready. Don't worry about a little wobble in the middle; brownies firm up as they cool.

Most baking recipes can be tested for doneness via the skewer or toothpick test; if a skewer plunged into the centre comes out clean, the bake is ready. Unfortunately, a skewer inserted into a brownie will nearly always emerge with a sexy cladding of crumbs – but that doesn't mean the test is entirely useless. A skewer covered in wet batter suggests the brownie is underbaked. Moist crumbs (especially ones that clump together when you press them between your fingers) are a good indication the brownie is ready.*

The golden rule of brownie-making is that underbaked is usually better than overbaked. But don't worry too much, because whatever you produce will be chocolatey and rich and delicious. There is really no such thing as a bad brownie.

brownie kit

Good news – you don't need lots of fancy equipment to make brownies and blondies. But the following bits and bobs will help.

the essentials

20cm square tin
Every brownie and blondie in this book has been tested in a 20cm square tin, with around 4cm high sides.** I recommend a loose-based tin, which makes it easier to lift out more fragile brownies. Ideally, choose a tin that is pale and lightweight (made from aluminium or similar) rather than heavy, dark metal; it will cook the brownies more evenly. You can use glass or ceramic dishes if that's all you have, but be aware the cooking time might be affected.

baking parchment
Always line the tin with baking parchment. It only takes a moment, and prevents frustration when you can't prise your brownies out. To line your tin, use a little oil or melted butter to grease the tin all over. Cut a square of baking parchment that's large enough to cover the sides as well as the base. Make diagonal cuts in each corner, then place the

*   If the skewer is completely clean, you've overbaked them, and should immediately eat them still warm with some remedial ice cream.
** Except the brownie-inspired recipes in chapter four, obviously. A brownie ice cream sundae feels wrong in a tin.

parchment onto the base of the tin and press the sides into place (you will have a little overlap on the corners).

electric whisk/balloon whisk
If you want that delectable papery crust on your brownies, you need to get some air into the batter (see Welcome to Brownie School, page 10). I recommend using an electric whisk, but you can also use an old-school balloon one and some welly – just whisk for a few extra minutes, or until your arm feels like it's about to fall off.

saucepan
Most of my brownies are prepared from start to finish in a saucepan – you melt the chocolate and butter together, then add the other ingredients. I use a medium-ish saucepan, around 20cm diameter; one with a heavy bottom is best.

sharp knife
An ordinary kitchen knife is all you need, but make sure it's sharp; the idea is to slice your brownies neatly, rather than crush them into crumbly defeat.

nice to have

measuring spoons
A set of measuring spoons is useful for accurately adding small quantities of salt, baking powder, vanilla extract and the like.

oven thermometer
Baking is a precise art, but ovens are imprecise – they often run slightly hotter or colder than they claim to, which can affect how well your brownies cook. An oven thermometer doesn't cost much and is invaluable in helping you check that you're baking at the right temperature.

silicon spatula
There's nothing wrong with a wooden spoon, but a silicon spatula is a brilliant all-rounder, whether you're folding in flour or mixing in chocolate chips. There is nothing quite as effective at scraping every last bit of batter out of the bowl.*

* Other than my husband, but there's only one of him.

brownie storecupboard

chocolate

Decent chocolate is key to a good brownie. Just like coq au vin will taste better if you use good wine, rather than that half-bottle of plonk that's been mostly vinegar since the eighth day of Christmas, a quality bar of chocolate will take your brownies from good to great.

Dark chocolate is the go-to for brownies. You don't need to spend a fortune – I tested most of this book using supermarket own-brand bars – but it is important that you use something around 70% 'cocoa solids' (you will find the information somewhere on the packaging). This means that 70% of the bar is made from cocoa beans. 70% chocolate will deliver a rich, deep flavour, and also ensure the recipe works; chocolate bars with less cocoa usually contain more of other ingredients like sugar, which can affect the success of the bake. Although chocolate purists will encourage you to buy bars without any additives, I find that chocolate which has 'emulsifier' in the list of ingredients (usually soy lecithin) can be a little more stable to bake with, with less chance of the chocolate splitting when you heat it.

Milk chocolate is less bitter than dark; as the name suggests, the intense cocoa is balanced by dairy, either in the form of powdered, liquid or condensed milk. Milk chocolate is delicious on its own, but can taste oddly bland in baked treats. This is why is why I usually combine it with a little dark. I recommend buying milk chocolate that contains at least 30% cocoa solids.

White chocolate is the star ingredient in blondies. It doesn't contain any cocoa solids, but lots of creamy cocoa butter, plus other ingredients such as dairy, sugar and vanilla. Good white chocolate will deliver a better flavour, but high quality is not as crucial as when making brownies. I successfully tested many blondies in this book with bars that were cheap as (chocolate) chips.

Talking of chocolate chips, for these you can use any type or percentage of chocolate you like. I prefer to hand-chop chocolate rather than buying ready-made chips, so you end up with a delicious combination of chunky pieces and delicate flakes.

butter and oil

Use proper butter, rather than a spread. Although putting salted butter on any available surface is my main extracurricular activity, for brownies I use unsalted – it means I can control the salt levels more easily, by adding to taste.

Some recipes in this book use a neutral-tasting oil, such as vegetable oil or coconut oil, instead of butter. Oils are vegan-friendly, and, because they have a less distinct flavour than butter, can help other ingredients shine through. Using oil can also create a slightly chewier brownie.

sugar

Sugar is crucial in brownies to balance the bitterness of the chocolate. You can use pretty much any variety, with deliciously different results. Caster sugar is the classic for brownies and is best for creating a papery crust; I sometimes swap it for golden caster, which brings a hint of toffee. For blondies, and some brownies, I mostly use light brown soft sugar; it has a butterscotch flavour and makes for a slightly moister bake. Light muscovado sugar is similar, with an even richer taste, while dark brown

sugar or treacle creates an intensely dark, molasses-y bake. Occasionally I'll use golden syrup, maple syrup or honey, each of which brings a unique flavour.

eggs

I use large eggs throughout this book (extra-large in the US). A large egg, in its shell, weighs between 63g and 73g. Egg size can have a drastic effect on your brownies, affecting everything from their moisture to their sturdiness. I weigh eggs before using; my go-to size is around 65g, but I try and make sure that if I'm adding an egg at the lower end of the spectrum – around 63g, for example – I use a larger one alongside it.*

flour

Like sugar, there's a wide world of flour beyond the classic white. Some of my recipes use wholemeal flour, or 'ancient grains' like rye and spelt, which have a pleasingly complex nuttiness. Now and again I use ground almonds in place of

* I'm a fun person to hang out with.

flour, which bring both flavour and moisture.

raising agents

As a general rule, I don't believe brownies have any business trying to go up in the world – they're best when dense and squishy. So, I don't use much in the way of raising agents, though now and again I'll add a smidgen of baking powder or self-raising flour if I want a cakier texture, or if there's lots of fresh fruit weighing the batter down. Blondies are a different matter, and can benefit from a little rise to alleviate that intensely sweet fudginess.

cocoa powder

A powerful weapon in the brownie lover's arsenal. Even if you're making a brownie with lots of dark chocolate, adding a few tablespoons of cocoa will make the bake more intensely chocolatey. Recipes that feature cocoa powder usually contain a little less flour, to prevent the brownies being too dry. You can make a ridiculously good brownie without any chocolate at all if you dial up the cocoa powder; see 'I don't have any chocolate' brownies on page 65.

salt

Always add salt to sweet recipes. It doesn't make your treats taste salty, but somehow enhances all the different flavours and brings them together. Salt is particularly good with chocolate, making it taste fuller and richer. I generally add at least a quarter of a teaspoon to my brownie mix, and sometimes as much as half a teaspoon. Fine sea salt is best for the batter, while crunchy sea salt flakes are good for sprinkling on top of the finished brownies, for an extra salty hit. If you need to be careful about your salt intake, feel free to leave it out – though a little pinch is better than none at all.

how to serve your brownies

A standard 20cm tin of brownies or blondies (the size used in this book) will yield 16 small squares or 9 big squares. The small size is better for coffee breaks and school cake sales. The latter is good if you're serving brownies for a dinner party dessert, or if you're down in the dumps and only a thwacking great brownie will persuade you out of them.

brownies for everyday

ultimate fudgy brownies
a classic for a reason

If I could only eat one brownie for the rest of my days, this would be it. Dark and rich, without nuts or other extras to distract from its bewitchingly oozy centre, I promise it will fill any hole in your life.

I have eaten these by myself in bed when I'm sad; dressed them up fancy with caramel sauce when I've got people round for dinner; sent chocolate-splotched packets off to family and friends; and exclaimed like a triumphant archaeologist when I excavate a forgotten stash from under the peas at the back of the freezer. This was the first recipe I developed for the book and though a mother should never have favourites, this one comes close.

200g unsalted butter,
    chopped into rough cubes,
    plus extra for greasing
300g dark chocolate
    (around 70% cocoa solids),
    roughly broken into pieces
300g caster sugar
3 large eggs and 1 large egg
    yolk, lightly beaten
50g plain flour
60g cocoa powder
½ teaspoon sea salt, plus
    extra to sprinkle

1   Preheat the oven to 180°C/160°C Fan/Gas Mark 4. Grease a 20cm square tin with a little butter and line with baking parchment.

2   Put the butter and chocolate in a medium saucepan over a low heat and melt together, stirring frequently, until combined. Stir in the sugar, then take off the heat. Leave to cool for 5 minutes or so, until warm to the touch rather than scalding hot.

3   Add the eggs to the pan and quickly stir to combine. Now beat, using a handheld electric whisk, on a medium-high speed, for about 3 minutes (alternatively, use a balloon whisk and some elbow grease); the mixture will become thick and velvety. This will help create a delicious crust.

4   Sift over the flour, cocoa powder and salt, and gently fold in with a spatula or large metal spoon until just combined. Transfer the mixture to your prepared tin – it will be rather thick – making sure to spread the mix into the corners. Bake for 30–35 minutes. The brownie should be set on top, with a few cracks around the edges. Let it cool in the tin for at least two hours before cutting into squares. I like these with a sprinkle of crunchy sea salt on top.

triple chocolate brownies
chocolate, chocolate and more chocolate

I don't know about you, but I'm a 'more is more' person. Extra sprinkles on a birthday cake; one more clove of garlic in the Bolognese; an olive *and* a twist of lemon in a martini. So, here is the souped-up version of my classic fudge brownie, dense with dark chocolate, and rippled with melting pockets of milk and white chocolate chips for that perfect balance of bitter and sweet.

200g unsalted butter,
    chopped into rough cubes,
    plus extra for greasing
200g dark chocolate
    (around 70% cocoa),
    roughly broken into pieces
300g caster sugar
3 large eggs, lightly beaten
60g plain flour
60g cocoa powder
½ teaspoon salt
80g white chocolate,
    chopped into chunks
80g milk chocolate,
    chopped into chunks

1   Preheat the oven to 180°C/160°C Fan/Gas Mark 4. Grease a 20cm square tin with a little butter and line with baking parchment.

2   Put the butter and dark chocolate in a medium saucepan over a low heat and melt together, stirring frequently, until combined. Stir in the sugar, then take off the heat. Leave to cool for 5 minutes or so, so the mix is just warm to the touch. (This is especially important for these brownies, as you don't want the chocolate chips to melt too much.)

3   Add the eggs to the pan and quickly stir to combine. Beat, using a handheld electric whisk, on a medium speed, for about 3 minutes (or go to town with a normal balloon whisk); the mixture should be as thick and glossy-looking as Willy Wonka's chocolate river.

4   Sift over the flour, cocoa powder and salt. Gently fold in with a spatula or large metal spoon. Add the chocolate chunks and stir in.

5   Transfer the mixture to your prepared tin, making sure to spread it into the corners, and bake for 35–40 minutes. The brownie should be set on top, with a few cracks around the edges. Let it cool in the tin completely before cutting into squares. I usually put these in the fridge for a few hours before cutting, especially if they're on the gooey side.

'I like cakey brownies'
one bowl, white chocolate drizzle

I was once very snobby about cakey brownies – my husband told me early in our relationship that he preferred them to fudgy, and I reacted a bit like he'd admitted he enjoyed eating hay. But today I am a better person, a brownie equal opportunist and a peacemaker, and a good cakey brownie will always find a home in my tin.

These brownies remind me of the kind I enjoyed as a child, a remnant of a time where bigger wasn't always better. They're not rich or showy, and are superb with a glass of cold milk. The recipe is a riff on a classic from the queen of British baking, Mary Berry, who probably wrote the first brownie recipe I ever made. It has the added virtue that it can all be made in one bowl.

130g unsalted butter, softened, plus extra for greasing
190g caster sugar
2 large eggs
60g self-raising flour
40g cocoa powder
¼ teaspoon salt
½ teaspoon vanilla paste or extract
100g dark or milk chocolate, chopped into small chunks
50g white chocolate, roughly chopped, for drizzling (optional)

1 Preheat the oven to 180°C/160°C Fan/Gas Mark 4. Grease a 20cm square tin with a little butter and line with baking parchment.

2 Put all the ingredients, except the chocolate, in a large bowl, and beat for 3–4 minutes with a handheld electric mixer (or a little longer with a wooden spoon) until the mixture is fluffy and smooth. Stir in the dark or milk chocolate chunks.

3 Spoon the mixture into the prepared tin, spreading it into the corners, and smooth with the back of a spoon. Bake for 40–45 minutes, until the top is set and crusty; you can cover with foil for the last 10–15 minutes if you think they are looking too browned. A skewer or toothpick plunged into the centre should come out clean, or with a few crumbs stuck to it. Leave in the tin to cool completely.

4 If making the drizzle, put the white chocolate in a heatproof bowl over a pan of just-simmering water, stirring to melt (alternatively, melt in a bowl in the microwave in 20-second bursts, stirring in-between). Use a spoon to drizzle the melted chocolate over the brownies, then let it harden before cutting into squares.

gentlemen prefer blondies
brown butter, white chocolate, vanilla

I spent the first three decades of my life loftily insisting that there was no point to blondies, but a few years ago I bit into one made by a friend and realised that perhaps blondes *do* have more fun.

In my defence, blondies are made with sweet white chocolate rather than intense dark, so it's easy for a blondie to taste sugary and flat. But a good one has an incredibly deep, almost butterscotch flavour.

I've given quite a large variation in cooking times, as even more so than with brownies, you need to trust your own judgement as to how fudgy or 'cooked' you want blondies to be (don't worry too much about this – after a batch or two, you'll work out exactly how long to bake them to suit your taste).

The trick to next-level blondies is to 'brown' the butter by cooking it until it is rich and nutty – I do this here, and any blondie recipe in this book (or, to be honest, most recipes in the world) would probably be improved by browning the butter first. But if this step sounds a bit cheffy or you don't have the time, feel free to skip. A tin of vanilla-speckled golden beauties will still be yours to enjoy.

240g light brown soft sugar
160g unsalted butter,
  chopped into rough cubes,
  plus extra for greasing
2 large eggs, lightly beaten
1½ teaspoons vanilla paste
  or extract
220g plain flour
½ teaspoon baking powder
½ teaspoon salt
180g white chocolate,
  chopped into small chunks

1   Preheat the oven to 180°C/160°C Fan/Gas Mark 4. Grease a 20cm square tin with a little butter and line with baking parchment. Put the sugar in a large bowl.

2   Melt the butter in a large pan on a low heat. To brown it, let the butter cook very gently, swirling the pan frequently, keeping a very careful eye on it. At first the butter will foam; after the foam subsides, the butter will start to turn golden brown and smell nutty. As soon as this happens, quickly remove the pan from the heat (the butter can burn very quickly) and pour into the bowl containing the sugar.

3 Mix the butter and sugar together, then add the eggs and vanilla and stir until smooth and combined. Sift in the flour, baking powder and salt, and very gently fold together. Stir in the white chocolate chunks.

4 Transfer the batter to the lined tin, spreading evenly to the edges and corners, and bake for 25–35 minutes, until golden and set on top, with only a faint jiggle in the middle (a shorter baking time will mean very gooey blondies; pushing to 35 minutes will give you a cakier result). Let them cool completely before eating. If you feel they're underbaked, refrigerate for a few hours before slicing.

first day on the job blondies

chai latte spices, milk chocolate puddles

There are three golden rules for starting a new job: iron your clothes, turn up on time and bring a home-made treat to sweeten up your colleagues.

Made by creaming butter with sugar, rather than the more conventional butter-melting method, these are a slightly cakier blondie, robust enough to survive the journey to the office. They're not too sweet, are gently spiced and should provide ample conversation material near the water cooler.

150g white chocolate, chopped into small chunks
100g unsalted butter, softened, chopped into rough cubes, plus extra for greasing
130g light brown soft sugar
50g demerara sugar
2 large eggs, lightly beaten
100g plain flour
1 teaspoon ground cinnamon
½ teaspoon ground ginger
½ teaspoon ground nutmeg
4 cardamom pods, seeds removed and crushed with a pestle and mortar
¼ teaspoon salt
80g pecans, roughly chopped
80–100g milk chocolate, roughly chopped into large shards (triangles look good)

1 Preheat the oven to 180°C/160°C Fan/Gas Mark 4. Grease a 20cm square tin with a little butter and line with baking parchment.

2 Melt 100g of the white chocolate in a heatproof bowl suspended over a pan of barely simmering water (alternatively, microwave in 20-second blasts, stirring in-between, until melted). Set aside to cool slightly.

3 Put the butter and both sugars in a large bowl, and beat together for a few minutes, ideally using a handheld electric whisk, until light and fluffy. Beat in the eggs, adding a little at a time, until combined. Add the cooled melted white chocolate and beat briefly to combine.

4 Sift in the flour, spices and salt, and use a spatula or large metal spoon to gently fold in. Mix in the pecans and the remaining 50g white chocolate chunks.

5 Transfer the mixture to the lined tin. Place the milk chocolate shards on top of the blondie. Bake until set on top and nicely golden – around 25–30 minutes (I usually take them out at the point when you shake the tin and they don't have much jiggle). Leave to cool before slicing.

tea and sympathy brownies

biscuits, milk chocolate, hint of tea

A friend who's having a bad day cannot fail to be cheered by a delivery of these; a hug in brownie form. There's something very nostalgic about them – they evoke the biscuit selection boxes of childhood, brought out at Christmas (which always provoked a fight over who got the jammy dodgers). The milk chocolate makes the brownies a little sweeter and mellower, while the brown sugar adds richness and warmth. You can leave out the tea if you like, but the hints of tannin complement the chocolate flavour.

200g unsalted butter, chopped into rough cubes, plus extra for greasing
3 English Breakfast teabags
150g dark chocolate (around 70% cocoa solids), finely chopped
100g milk chocolate, finely chopped
150g golden caster sugar
100g light brown soft sugar
3 large eggs
1 teaspoon vanilla paste or extract
80g plain flour
40g cocoa powder
¼ teaspoon salt
8–9 assorted favourite biscuits, such as Rich Tea and Bourbons

1 Preheat the oven to 180°C/160°C Fan/Gas Mark 4. Grease a 20cm square tin with a little butter and line with baking parchment.

2 Melt the butter in a large saucepan over a low heat. Snip open the teabags and tip the leaves into the pan. Take off the heat and leave for 10–15 minutes to infuse. Now pour the butter through a sieve into a fresh saucepan. Use a spoon to gently press the tea leaves left behind in the sieve to extract as much butter as possible. (Don't worry if some smaller tea leaves pass through the sieve.)

3 Put this saucepan on a low heat, add both types of chocolate and stir until melted and smooth. Take off the heat, stir in both of the sugars, and leave to cool for a few minutes.

4 Add the eggs and vanilla to the pan. Beat, ideally using a handheld electric whisk on a medium speed, for about 3 minutes, until thick and smooth.

5 Sift over the flour, cocoa powder and salt, and gently fold in until just combined. Transfer the mixture to your prepared tin and spread to the edges and into the corners. Place your biscuits on top of the mix and very gently press in. (I usually remove the bottom layer of sandwich biscuits, such as custard creams, so as not to weigh down the mix too much. They also provide a handy mid-recipe snack.)

6   Bake for 40–50 minutes; the exact time may vary slightly depending on the size and type of biscuits. The brownie should be set on top, with a few cracks around the edges, but still with a little wobble in the centre. Cool in the tin completely before cutting into squares. Put the kettle on and decide who gets the jammy dodger corner.

netflix and chilli brownies
popcorn, ginger, a touch of chilli

A brownie is foolproof date food. Nearly everyone likes them; they show you've made an effort, but in a casual 'Oh I just whipped up these up while wearing matching underwear' kind of way; and an unusual flavour plants the seed that you're interesting enough to see again. Most importantly, they're ideal for sharing on the sofa.

As befits a tool of seduction, these are graduates of the decadently fudgy school of brownie, but I've turned up the heat with ginger and chilli and added popcorn for a movie night feel. Ancho chilli bring a gentle, fruity heat, but you can use normal chilli (just use half as much) or leave it out.

200g unsalted butter, chopped into rough cubes, plus extra for greasing
200g dark chocolate (around 70% cocoa solids), roughly broken into pieces
150g caster sugar
150g light muscovado sugar
80g crunchy toffee popcorn, such as Butterkist
3 large eggs, lightly beaten
60g plain flour
60g cocoa powder
1 teaspoon ancho chilli flakes
¼ teaspoon salt
60g stem ginger, chopped, plus 1 tablespoon syrup from the jar
½ small red chilli, deseeded and finely chopped, to garnish (optional)

1 Preheat the oven to 180°C/160°C Fan/Gas Mark 4. Grease a 20cm square tin with a little butter and line with baking parchment.

2 Put the butter and chocolate in a medium saucepan and place over a low heat. Cook, stirring, until smooth and melted. Take off the heat, add the sugars and stir until smooth. Set aside and let cool for at least 5 minutes.

3 Meanwhile, put the popcorn into a plastic bag, and bash roughly with the end of a rolling pin, so you have some bigger and some smaller chunks.*

4 Add the eggs to the chocolate mix and stir until glossy and combined. Sift over the flour, cocoa powder and salt, add the chilli flakes, and gently fold together. Fold in the stem ginger and syrup and most of the popcorn.

5 Transfer the mixture to the prepared tin. Scatter the remaining popcorn on top, pressing them into the batter slightly. Bake for 45–50 minutes (cover with foil after 20 minutes if it looks like the popcorn is catching), until set on top and there's no movement; a skewer inserted will still come out rather wet. Leave the brownies cool before slicing. Scatter over the red chilli before serving, if liked. Offer to your date with ice cream and a smile.

* It's quite therapeutic to picture an ex as you smash.

here comes summer brownies

strawberries, marshmallows, wafers

I love summer. The clink of ice cubes in that first glass of Pimm's; the smell of barbecue that drifts over the neighbourhood, gently infusing your laundry with a whiff of sausages.

A few summers back, I needed to take a dessert to a barbecue, one that would please adults and children alike, and wondered if I could create a brownie to rival standard summer puds like pavlova and Eton mess. This was the answer – a satisfying chocolate base, topped with fluffy strawberry mousse and decorated with crushed ice cream wafers. Adding marshmallows to the mousse is a good trick – not only do they bring a sweet, creamy flavour, but they help the mousse set without the need to faff about with gelatine or eggs.

for the brownie base

130g unsalted butter, chopped into rough cubes, plus extra for greasing
100g dark chocolate (around 70% cocoa solids), roughly broken into pieces
2 large eggs
180g caster sugar
90g plain flour
¼ teaspoon salt

for the strawberry mallow mousse

300g strawberries
20g caster sugar
zest of 1 lemon, juice of ½
150g mini marshmallows
200ml double cream, whipped

1 Preheat the oven to 180°C/160°C Fan/Gas Mark 4. Grease a 20cm square tin, ideally a high-sided one with a loose base (this makes the brownies easier to remove), with a little butter and line with baking parchment.

2 Melt the butter and chocolate together in a medium saucepan over a low heat, stirring frequently until combined. Leave to cool slightly, until the mix is warm to the touch rather than hot.

3 Whisk the eggs and sugar lightly together in a bowl, just until combined, then stir into the chocolate-butter mixture until smooth. Sift over the flour and salt, and gently fold together.

4 Transfer to the tin and bake for around 15–20 minutes until set on top, and a skewer inserted into the middle comes out with moist crumbs. Let it cool completely before making the strawberry mousse (you can pop the brownie in the fridge to speed this part up if needed).

*handful of white chocolate
  chunks*
*1–2 ice cream wafers
  or cones*

5 To make the mousse, first set aside two large strawberries (about 50g) for the decoration. Hull and roughly chop the rest and put them in a saucepan over a medium heat with the sugar and lemon juice. Stir to start dissolving the sugar and cook for 5–10 minutes until the strawberries are soft and breaking down. Remove from the heat and mash to a rough purée, using a fork or masher, then add the marshmallows. Stir vigorously until they've completely dissolved – this may take a few minutes. (If the marshmallows are stubbornly refusing to melt, you can put the pan briefly back over a low heat to encourage them.) Set aside to cool.

6 Whip the cream in a large bowl until soft peaks form. Scrape the cooled strawberry marshmallow mixture into the bowl, along with the lemon zest, and fold to combine. The mousse will be quite wet, so transfer the bowl to the fridge for 30 minutes or so to help it set slightly.

7 Once the mousse has firmed up a little, spoon it over the brownie, and smooth into an even layer. Slice the reserved strawberries into thin slices and scatter over the top, along with the white chocolate chunks. Refrigerate for at least 2 hours until set.

8 To serve, carefully remove the brownie from the tin (the mousse will be quite delicate) and unpeel the baking parchment. Break up the ice cream wafers into rough pieces, and scatter over the top, pressing in gently with your hands. Enjoy before the wasps do.

'did I mention I'm a vegan?' brownies

coconut oil, muscovado sugar, almond milk

It took me many attempts to crack a decent vegan brownie – by which I mean the kind of brownie that everyone at the table will enjoy eating, not a sad individual square you pass to your vegan friend with an apologetic smile.

The secret ingredient here is flaxseed, which is now widely available in health food shops and bigger supermarkets. When combined with water, they create a thick paste which helps hold the brownie together, a little like eggs do.

3 tablespoons ground flaxseed
80g coconut oil, plus extra for greasing
200g vegan dark chocolate (around 70% cocoa solids), roughly broken into pieces
230g light muscovado sugar
2 teaspoons vanilla paste or extract
½ teaspoon instant coffee granules, dissolved in 1 tablespoon boiling water
130ml almond or other plant milk
160g plain flour
40g cocoa powder
½ teaspoon baking powder
¼ teaspoon salt
80g vegan dark, milk or white chocolate, chopped into small chunks

1   Preheat the oven to 180°C/160°C Fan/Gas Mark 4. Grease a 20cm square tin with a little oil and line with baking parchment.

2   Put the flaxseed in a mug or bowl, add 7 tablespoons of cold water, and give it a good stir. Leave to one side.

3   Put the coconut oil and chocolate in a medium saucepan set over a low heat, stirring regularly, until melted. Leave to cool for 5 minutes or so, until just warm to the touch.

4   Stir in the sugar. Add the vanilla, coffee, flaxseed mixture and almond milk and stir until smooth. Sift over the flour, cocoa powder, baking powder and salt, and gently fold together. Stir through the chocolate chunks.

5   Transfer the mixture to the prepared tin and spread to the edges. Bake for 25–30 minutes, until set on top, with a few cracks appearing around the edges. Don't worry if there's still movement when you shake the tin; you want to avoid overbaking these, as this makes them dry and crumbly. Let the brownie cool completely before cutting into squares. These are good with ice cream (vegan, obviously).

'did I mention I can't eat gluten?' brownies

ground almonds, lots of chocolate

A recipe for those occasions when someone drops the 'I can't eat gluten' bombshell. Brownies can be easily adapted to work without flour; they're so heavy and squidgy that they don't rely on gluten for structure in the same needy way a cake or bread does, though you do need to add a little something (other than your anxious hopes and prayers) to help hold them together.

I'm not a big fan of gluten-free flour – most seem to have a slightly grainy texture – so I use a mix of ground almonds and cornflour instead. The almonds bring moistness and faint nuttiness, while the cornflour (an idea from food writer Felicity Cloake) helps bind the mixture while being neutral-tasting enough to let the chocolate take centre stage. I'd be surprised if anyone guesses these are a flour-free zone.

200g unsalted butter,
    chopped into rough cubes,
    plus extra for greasing
300g dark chocolate
    (around 70% cocoa solids),
    roughly broken into pieces
280g caster sugar
3 large eggs
50g ground almonds
60g cornflour
½ teaspoon salt

1   Preheat the oven to 180°C/160°C Fan/Gas Mark 4. Grease a 20cm square tin with a little butter and line with baking parchment.

2   Put the butter and chocolate in a medium saucepan and set over a low heat, stirring frequently, until melted together. Stir in the sugar, then take off the heat. Leave to cool for 5 minutes or so, so the mixture is just warm to the touch.

3   Add the eggs to the pan and quickly stir to combine. Beat, using a handheld electric whisk on a medium speed, for about 3 minutes, until thick and velvety (or a few minutes longer with a balloon whisk).

4   Add the ground almonds, cornflour and salt, and gently fold in.

5   Transfer the mixture to your prepared tin. Bake for around 35 minutes. The brownie should be set on top, with a few cracks around the edges, and there shouldn't be any wobble when you shake the tin. Let it cool in the tin for a few hours before cutting into squares.

'I should eat more vegetables' brownies

carrot, spices, cream cheese

A cross between a brownie and a carrot cake. The carrot brings sweetness and moisture, the wholemeal flour adds nuttiness and the cream cheese icing is pleasingly tangy.

The candied carrot curls are completely optional, but are a nice finishing touch – and an excellent opportunity to use up that last floppy carrot in the vegetable drawer. These are also good made with rye or spelt flour.

200g unsalted butter, chopped into rough cubes, plus extra for greasing
200g dark chocolate (around 70% cocoa solids), roughly broken into pieces
150g light brown soft sugar
100g caster sugar
3 large eggs, lightly beaten
120g wholemeal flour
1 teaspoon ground cinnamon, plus extra to decorate if liked
¼ teaspoon ground nutmeg
¼ teaspoon salt
½ teaspoon baking powder
1 large carrot (about 150g), peeled and grated
zest of 1 orange, plus 1 tablespoon juice
80g walnuts, roughly chopped, plus a few extra to decorate if liked
60g sultanas

for the candied carrot curls (optional)
100g caster sugar, plus 1 tablespoon

1   Preheat the oven to 180°C/160°C Fan/Gas Mark 4. Grease a 20cm square tin with a little butter and line with baking parchment.

2   Put the butter and chocolate in a medium saucepan set over a low heat and melt together, stirring frequently, until combined. Stir in the sugars, then take off the heat. Leave to cool for 5 minutes or so, until warm to the touch rather than hot.

3   Add the eggs to the pan and mix in until smooth. Sift over the flour, spices, salt and baking powder, and add the grated carrot, orange zest and juice, walnuts and sultanas. Gently mix everything together.

4   Transfer to your prepared tin, making sure to spread into the edges and corners. Bake for 30 minutes. The brownie should be set on top, with a few cracks around the edges, and not much movement in the centre. Put it back in the oven for an extra 3–5 minutes if it feels very jiggly, or you'd rather it was on the cakier side. Leave the oven on if making the carrot curls, and let the brownies cool in the tin.

5   To make the curls, line a baking tray with baking parchment. Put the 100g of sugar in a small-medium-sized saucepan with 100ml of water and heat gently, stirring to dissolve the sugar. Once the sugar has dissolved, add the carrot strips to the sugar syrup –

1 carrot, peeled into
   long strips

for the cream cheese icing
200g full-fat soft cheese
50g unsalted butter,
   softened
60g icing sugar, sifted

they should just be covered. Turn up the heat and boil for 5 minutes.

6   Carefully remove the carrot strips with tongs and put them on the lined baking tray. Transfer to the oven and cook for around 7–10 minutes, depending on how thick they are. Remove from the oven and use tongs to arrange them on a cooling rack. If you like, you can shape them into curls by twisting around a chopstick or handle of a wooden spoon – work swiftly and carefully, because they harden very fast but will also be hot. Sprinkle with the remaining tablespoon of caster sugar and leave to cool and crisp up further for at least 20 minutes.

7   To make the cream cheese icing, combine the ingredients in a bowl and whisk briefly until smooth. Spread the icing on top of the brownies, then decorate with the candied carrot curls, plus an extra sprinkling of cinnamon and a few pecans, if liked.

sunday blondies

apples, custard, crumble

There is no happier way to spend a Sunday afternoon than a roast dinner with family or friends, followed by a big bowl of pudding.* My mum worked on Sundays throughout most of my childhood, and our dinner was always pushed back into the evening so she could join us. To this day, Sunday lunch in the afternoon feels special.

This is a blondie/cake hybrid, inspired by my favourite post-roast dessert, apple crumble and custard. I like to eat it warm with extra custard, or a scoop of ice cream.

2 eating apples, cored and chopped into 1.5cm chunks (about 200g chopped apple)
170g plain flour, plus 1 tablespoon
150g unsalted butter, chopped into rough cubes, plus extra for greasing
180g light brown soft sugar
2 large eggs, lightly beaten
1 teaspoon vanilla paste or extract
60g custard powder
1 teaspoon baking powder
½ teaspoon salt
100g white chocolate, chopped into small chunks

for the crumble topping
60g plain flour
40g caster sugar
½ teaspoon cinnamon
pinch of salt
30g unsalted cold butter, cut into small pieces

1   Preheat the oven to 180°C/160°C Fan/Gas Mark 4. Grease a 20cm square tin with a little butter and line with baking parchment. Toss the apple chunks in a bowl with the 1 tablespoon of flour.

2   Put all the ingredients for the crumble topping, except the butter, in a bowl and stir together. Take a few cubes of butter at a time and gently rub the butter into the flour, until you have what looks like breadcrumbs. Put to one side while you make the blondie.

3   Melt the butter in a medium saucepan on a low heat. Let it cool for 5 minutes. Stir in the sugar, then mix in the eggs and vanilla. Sift in the flour, custard powder and baking powder, add the salt, and gently fold together until just combined. Stir in the white chocolate and the flour-coated apple chunks.

4   Transfer the mix to your lined tin, then scatter the crumble topping over the top. Bake for 40–45 minutes, until the blondie feels set (it shouldn't jiggle when you shake the tin) and a skewer inserted comes out with moist crumbs.

*   Followed, in turn, by a light bout of indigestion on the sofa.

'fancy a pint?' brownies

stout, treacle, peanuts

Beer and chocolate are classic drinking buddies – they bring out each other's dark, bitter qualities.* Chocolate cakes made with stout have been around for years, but here I've given the idea a brownie makeover, adding that classic pub snack, peanuts, for a little salty crunch.

330ml bottle stout, such as Guinness
200g unsalted butter, chopped into rough cubes, plus extra for greasing
250g dark chocolate (around 70% cocoa solids), roughly broken into pieces
200g light brown soft sugar
3 tablespoons treacle
3 large eggs, lightly beaten
30g cocoa powder
120g plain flour
pinch of salt (optional)
80g roasted salted peanuts, roughly chopped, plus a handful extra to decorate

for the cream cheese icing
250g cream cheese (I use Philadelphia as other brands can be a little thin)
120g icing sugar
150 double cream

1   Preheat the oven to 180°C/160°C Fan/Gas Mark 4. Grease a 20cm square tin with a little butter and line with baking parchment.

2   Pour the stout into a large saucepan and bring to the boil. Turn down the heat and let it bubble gently for 10–15 minutes, until thickened and reduced by half. Keep an eye on it; if the beer gets too hot, it can foam up. You should end up with about 160ml.

3   Add the butter and the chocolate to the pan and cook, stirring frequently, until melted together and combined. Stir in the sugar and treacle. Add the eggs and mix well. Sift over the flour and cocoa powder, and gently fold in, along with a pinch of salt if liked. Stir in the peanuts.

4   Transfer the mixture – it will be quite thin – to your tin and bake for 35–40 minutes. The brownie should be set on top, with a few cracks around the edge, and will leave some crumbs on a skewer. Let it cool completely in the tin.

5   To make the icing, put the cream cheese and icing sugar in a large bowl and beat briefly together until smooth. Add the double cream and whip (ideally using a handheld electric whisk) until it is thick but spreadable; you may need to do this for a good minute or so. Remove the brownie from the tin and place on a board. Spoon on the icing and use a knife to create loose waves, like the foamy head of a beer. Sprinkle over the remaining nuts.

*   We've all got a dangerous pub friend like that.

ready for instagram blondies

pistachios, rose, waiting for their close-up

A beautiful blondie that will turn heads on social media. It tastes as striking as it looks, flecked with creamy, bright-green pistachios and scattered with rose petals.

Be cautious with the amount of rosewater you add; different brands vary in intensity, and some people prefer a subtle hint to a bungee jump into pot-pourri.

160g unsalted butter, chopped into rough cubes, plus extra for greasing
140g plain flour
80g ground almonds
½ teaspoon baking powder
5 cardamom pods, seeds crushed
½ teaspoon salt
240g light brown soft sugar
2 large eggs, lightly beaten
1 teaspoon vanilla paste or extract
½–1 teaspoon concentrated rosewater
100g white chocolate, chopped into small chunks
100g pistachios, roughly chopped
extra pistachios and rose petals to garnish (optional)

1 Preheat the oven to 180°C/160°C Fan/Gas Mark 4. Grease a 20cm square tin with a little butter and line with baking parchment.

2 Melt the butter in a medium saucepan over a low heat. Leave for 5–10 minutes to cool slightly. Meanwhile, sift the flour into a bowl and stir in the ground almonds, baking powder, cardamom and salt.

3 Add the sugar to the pan containing the melted butter and stir to combine, then add the eggs, vanilla and rosewater. Stir together to make a smooth, glossy mixture. Add the flour mixture to the pan, and gently fold in. Add the white chocolate chunks and two-thirds of the pistachios and stir to combine. Spoon the mixture into the prepared tin, making sure to spread to the edges and into the corners. Scatter the reserved pistachios on top.

4 Bake for 28–35 minutes, until golden and set on top; there should still be a little movement in the centre. Let it cool completely in the tin. Garnish with more pistachios and rose petals, if liked. Take a few photographs for your Instagram, then enjoy.

'I need a holiday' blondies

apricots, honey, thyme

This is a recipe for when you're dreaming of escape. I invented it in 2020, while stuck at home due to Covid-19. I kept fantasising about France – and in particular, Provence, with its lavender fields and golden farmhouses, soaked in sunshine like a chunk of bread dipped in olive oil. This result was a celebration of some of my favourite Provençal flavours.*

The thyme might sound unusual, but it brings a hint of aromatic savouriness; rosemary or lavender also work well. This is a cakier blondie, which I like to serve still slightly warm as a pudding, with ice cream, a drizzle of honey and a cold glass of pale rosé.

2–3 apricots (smaller, firmer
    ones work best)
150g unsalted butter,
    chopped into rough cubes,
    plus extra for greasing
100g white chocolate,
    roughly broken into pieces
2 large eggs, lightly beaten
½ teaspoon vanilla paste
    or extract
150g light brown soft sugar
50g honey, plus extra
    to serve
180g plain flour
½ teaspoon baking powder
¼ teaspoon salt
6–7 bushy sprigs of thyme

1   Preheat the oven to 180°C/160°C Fan/Gas Mark 4. Grease a 20cm square tin with a little butter and line with baking parchment.

2   Halve and stone the apricots, then thinly slice. If the fruit is very juicy, rest briefly on kitchen paper to absorb a little of the liquid.

3   Melt the butter and white chocolate together in a medium saucepan over a low heat, stirring occasionally. Take off the heat and leave to cool for 10 minutes or so.

4   Add the eggs and vanilla and mix to make a smooth batter. Stir in the sugar and the honey. Sift over the flour, baking powder and salt, and fold together.

5   Transfer the mixture to the prepared tin. Arrange the sliced apricots over the top – I like to fan them out in groups of 3–4 slices, making sure to leave some gaps between them. Gently place the thyme sprigs in these gaps; I like to use the whole sprigs but you could sprinkle picked leaves if you prefer. Bake for 28–33 minutes, until golden and set on top (there may still be a slight wobble in the centre). Let it cool a little. Serve drizzled with extra honey, raising a glass towards France.

*   There is an excellent German word, *fernweh*, which means 'farsickness', longing for far-off places. There is, sadly, not a word for 'so farsick I made a blondie in tribute'.

'I like to recycle' brownies

spent coffee, condensed milk

Brownies aren't just delicious; they can help save the world.* I came up with this eco-friendly number as a way to reinvent the soggy coffee grounds at the bottom of my cafetiere, rather than scraping them into the bin.

The addition of condensed milk is inspired by one of my favourite summer drinks, Vietnamese iced coffee, where the sweet milk balances the bitter coffee. Here, I've used condensed milk to create a gooey middle and a sticky, burnished, almost caramelised swirl on top, which offsets the slightly cakey brownie.

If you don't have leftover coffee grounds, you can use instant coffee instead. Just dissolve 2 tablespoons in 3–4 tablespoons boiling water when you start making the brownies, leave to cool, then stir it in after you've added the flour.

1 x 397g tin sweetened condensed milk
120g unsalted butter, chopped into rough cubes, plus extra for greasing
150g dark chocolate (around 70% cocoa solids), roughly broken into pieces
200g light brown soft sugar
2 large eggs, lightly beaten
1 teaspoon vanilla paste or extract
50g used coffee grounds (finely ground or espresso is best)
100g plain flour
¼ teaspoon salt

1 A few hours before you want to make the brownie, or ideally the night before, pop the condensed milk tin in the fridge. (This helps ensure you get a nice thick layer in the brownie, rather than it melting away into the batter.)

2 Preheat the oven to 180°C/160°C Fan/Gas Mark 4. Grease a 20cm square tin with a little butter and line with baking parchment.

3 Put the butter and chocolate in a medium saucepan over a low heat, stirring regularly, until melted together. Stir in the sugar and 3 tablespoons of the condensed milk, then take off the heat. Leave for 10 minutes to cool slightly.

4 Add the eggs and vanilla and mix to create a smooth batter. Stir in the coffee grounds. Sift in the flour and salt, and gently fold in.

* Not scientifically proven.

5   Transfer half the mixture to the tin and spread it out evenly. Weigh 100g of the condensed milk into a bowl, and use a dessert spoon to evenly dollop this over the brownie mix. Try to leave a roughly 2cm border around the edges if you can.

6   Carefully spoon over the rest of batter, covering the condensed milk. Now dollop over the remaining condensed milk from the tin (I usually have about 190g left at this point), again leaving a border around the edge. Use a knife to gently swirl the condensed milk into the brownie mix – I only swirl a little, disturbing just the top half of the brownie mix, as I find this is the best way to create fat, gooey pockets of the milk.

7   Bake for around 40 minutes until the brownie is set on top and the condensed milk swirl looks caramelised and golden-brown; there may still be a little wobble in the brownies' centre. Let it cool completely before serving.

8   These are exceptionally gooey – especially when that condensed milk centre oozes out – so put the brownies in the fridge if you want an easier slicing experience.

a bite-sized history of brownies

The Romans gave the world underfloor heating. China invented paper. When future civilisations study the achievements of the United States, I hope they acknowledge that its greatest contribution was the brownie.*

Although brownies seem as baked into American culture as cupcakes and apple pie, it was only a little over a century ago that they began leaving crumbs over the nation's kitchens. Chocolate, as a bitter and not entirely pleasant drink, was well-established in the US by the seventeenth century; it had an even longer history in Latin America, where it played an important role in Mayan and Aztec cultures. But it wasn't until the 1800s, when sweetened solid chocolate and cocoa powder became more widely available and affordable, that cooks began baking chocolate-flavoured treats.

Like many great recipes, brownies' exact origins are murky. Some say they were invented in 1893 at a Chicago hotel, when the wealthy socialite Bertha Potter Palmer asked the chef to create a simple, easily-transportable cake that could be popped into the lunch boxes of her female friends attending a nearby exposition. (She must have got a hefty dry-cleaning bill and some side-eye for all those chocolate-smeared dresses.) Others link them to Bangor in Maine, claiming they were invented there by one Mildred Brown Schrumpf (her nickname: 'Brownie'), or by an anonymous housewife who messed up a chocolate cake, only for her guests to rave about the result.

What we do know is that the by the end of the twentieth century, brownie recipes had started popping up in cookbooks. They didn't always bear much resemblance to the rich slabs of goo we're used to today. Most were rather frugal in the chocolate department; one of the first recipes – from the 1896 *Boston Cooking-School Cook Book* – cheekily didn't contain a scrap of chocolate at all, but was instead flavoured with 'Porto Rico molasses'.**

As the US emerged from the Second World War, it entered a new period of prosperity. People developed a taste for richer, sweeter, more

---

* I will concede the moon landing was also quite important.
** Although the word 'blondie' doesn't appear until the 1980s, this interestingly suggests that the first brownies might have been closer to a blondie in flavour.

indulgent foods, and brownies rose magnificently (or sank fudgily) to the task. But what really made the brownie a household name was the arrival of ready-made brownie mixes, pioneered by food companies such as General Mills and Pillsbury, and heavily promoted via cooking booklets and events. These 'box brownies' seduced families with their promise of delicious home-baked goods without any stress. Soon every kitchen in the country had a box or two in the cupboard. To this day, the nostalgic taste of brownies from a box mix triggers Americans' taste buds so powerfully, many prefer them to any other sort.

At the other end of the scale, of course, there were artisan bakeries, who showed how superlative a homemade brownie or blondie could be – especially when made with the best-quality chocolate, and enough butter to make your doctor wince. By the 1990s, brownies had made chocolatey inroads into other countries, including the UK, where they began to appear on coffee shop counters, squidging temptingly against the glass, making British staples like poor old carrot cake look rather dull in comparison.

Rich and indulgent, yet comforting and homely, brownies are that rare treat that pleases everyone, bringing a table together. It's no surprise that in the 1994 film *Notting Hill*, it's a jokey dinner party fight over who deserves 'the last brownie' that finally triggers Julia Roberts' fragile film star to talk about her past.

My favourite brownie story comes from New York in the 1980s, when a young woman and her father befriended their elderly neighbour – who happened to be the great American actor Katherine Hepburn. After hearing she'd been in a car accident, they kindly dropped off a batch of homemade brownies. The movie star took one bite, only to shout 'Too much flour!' and insist they scribble down her recipe. Writing in *The New York Times* many years later, the daughter said she would always be grateful to Hepburn 'for giving me these rules to live by: 1. Never quit. 2. Be yourself. 3. Don't put too much flour in your brownies.'

brownies
for comfort

friday night brownies

red wine, chocolate ganache

My favourite moment in the week is unlocking the front door on a Friday night. I grab a glass of red wine and some chocolate, then collapse into the sofa with such enthusiasm the cat pops over to check that I'm alright.* Even if there's laundry to sort and I've got to invent dinner from the single parsnip and half-jar of gherkins in the fridge, it doesn't matter. This brownie was inspired by that Friday-night feeling.

for the brownie
200ml vegetable oil, plus extra for greasing
150g dark chocolate (around 70% cocoa solids), roughly broken into pieces
100g dark brown soft sugar
150g caster sugar
2 large eggs and 1 large egg yolk, lightly beaten
100ml red wine (something fruity works well)
120g plain flour
50g cocoa powder
½ teaspoon salt

for the ganache topping
100g milk chocolate, finely chopped
100g dark chocolate, finely chopped
100ml double cream
1 tablespoon unsalted butter
red grapes and chocolate squares, to decorate (optional)

1 Preheat the oven to 180°C/160°C Fan/Gas Mark 4. Grease a 20cm square tin with a little oil and line with baking parchment.

2 Put the oil and chocolate in a heatproof bowl over a pan of barely simmering water and melt together, stirring frequently, until combined. Take off the heat, let it cool for a few minutes, then stir in the sugars. Add the eggs and mix thoroughly. Pour in the wine, sift over the flour, cocoa powder and salt, and mix until smooth.

3 Transfer the mixture to your prepared tin. Bake for 30–35 minutes. The brownie should be set on top, with a few cracks around the edges. Leave in the tin until cool.

4 To make the ganache, put the chocolate in a large bowl. Put the cream and butter in a saucepan and heat gently until simmering, stirring occasionally to help the butter melt. Pour over the chocolate. Leave for a minute so the chocolate starts melting, then whisk until you have a smooth, glossy mixture. (If the chocolate is refusing to melt, give the bowl a very quick blast in the microwave.) Let it cool until it's thick and spreadable; I sometimes pop the bowl in the fridge to speed this up.

5 Spread the ganache over the brownie and decorate with grapes (I slice mine thinly) and chocolate squares, if liked.

* Wine experts will tell you that wine and chocolate don't go together well, and I'm sure they're right, but thankfully I've never spotted one in my living room.

'I don't have any chocolate' brownies

cocoa powder, no fuss

This is a recipe for when there's no chocolate in the house, and you have to improvise with store cupboard ingredients. These are loosely adapted from American food writer Alice Medrich's recipe. It is my husband's favourite brownie, which is quite annoying considering how many of mine he has tried over the years.

You will not believe, the first time you make these, that they don't contain a scrap of chocolate. The cocoa gives them an intense chocolatey-ness, and they have a chewy quality, too. I add a little coffee, which heightens their flavour without making them taste at all of coffee, but you can leave it out if preferred.

140g unsalted butter, chopped into rough cubes, plus extra for greasing
250g caster sugar
80g cocoa powder, plus extra to dust
¼ teaspoon salt
2 large eggs
1 tablespoon instant coffee powder, dissolved in 1 tablespoon boiling water (optional)
70g plain flour

1 Preheat the oven to 180°C/160°C Fan/Gas Mark 4. Grease a 20cm square tin with a little butter and line with baking parchment.

2 Combine the butter, sugar, cocoa powder and salt in a medium saucepan over a low heat. Stir together until melted; don't worry if the mixture looks unappetisingly gritty. Remove from the heat and allow to cool for a few minutes.

3 Add the eggs one at a time, stirring vigorously to mix. Once combined, stir in the coffee if using, then sift in the flour. Beat again vigorously until you have a smooth, shiny mixture.

4 Transfer to the prepared tin and bake for 20–25 minutes. Let it cool, and dust with a little extra cocoa powder if liked before serving.

'cheating on brownies with cookies' brownies

brownie base, cookie dough top

This recipe was born one quiet, rainy Saturday afternoon when I couldn't work out if I wanted brownies or cookies. With the self-assurance of Neil Armstrong and Buzz Aldrin planting their flag on the moon, I crowned a tin of brownies with a layer of chocolate chip cookie dough, and haven't felt bad about being indecisive since. If you don't want to use raw egg in the cookie dough, replace it with 3 tablespoons of whole milk. You'll need 40g less flour.

for the brownie

200g unsalted butter,
    chopped into rough cubes,
    plus extra for greasing
200g dark chocolate
    (around 70% cocoa solids),
    roughly broken into pieces
270g caster sugar
3 large eggs, lightly beaten
80g plain flour
50g cocoa powder
¼ teaspoon salt

for the cookie dough

150g unsalted butter,
    at room temperature
160g light brown soft sugar
60g caster sugar
1 large egg, lightly beaten
1 tablespoon vanilla paste
    or extract
220g plain flour
¼ teaspoon salt
120g milk chocolate,
    chopped into small chunks

1 Preheat the oven to 180°C/160°C Fan/Gas Mark 4. Grease a 20cm square tin, ideally a high-sided one with a loose base (this makes the brownies easier to remove), with a little butter and line with baking parchment.

2 Melt the butter and chocolate together in a medium saucepan over a low heat, stirring regularly, until combined. Take off the heat, stir in the sugar and leave to cool slightly, until warm to the touch rather than hot.

3 Add the eggs and mix well until combined. Sift over the flour, cocoa powder and salt, and gently fold together. Transfer to the tin and bake for 25–30 minutes until set on top. Let it cool for as long as possible – it doesn't need to be completely cold, but the cookie dough layer will melt if the brownie beneath is too warm.

4 To make the cookie dough, put the butter and both sugars in a large bowl and beat, ideally using a handheld electric whisk, until combined and fluffy – I give it at least 3 minutes. Add the egg and the vanilla extract and beat until combined. Sift in the flour and salt and combine with a spatula or large metal spoon until it comes together into a smooth dough. Fold in the chocolate chunks. Eat a little bit while nobody is watching.

5 Spread the cookie dough evenly over the brownie, and press down to make a smooth, firm layer (I use my hands instead of a spoon). Chill in the fridge for at least 2 hours, so the cookie dough firms up, before cutting into squares.

'can I have brownies for breakfast?' brownies

nutella, banana, cereal crunch

Yes, you can – especially if you incorporate breakfast staples like Nutella and banana into the mix. Hazelnut spreads work well in brownies; they provide a nutty richness and deep cocoa flavour, which means you don't need to add any chocolate at all.

The cereal layer is inspired by one of my favourite childhood treats, fridge cake. If you prefer, you can leave it off, but I love the combo of sticky brownie and crunchy topping.*

for the brownie

100g dried banana chips
    (you could also use raisins
    or hazelnuts)
80g unsalted butter,
    softened and chopped
    into rough cubes, plus
    extra for greasing
100g caster sugar
2 large eggs, lightly beaten
300g Nutella or another
    hazelnut spread
60g plain flour
40g cocoa powder
¼ teaspoon salt

for the cereal crunch
    topping

150g milk chocolate, roughly
    chopped
80g unsalted butter
40g golden syrup
100g mixed favourite cereals
    (such as cornflakes and
    puffed rice)

1 Preheat the oven to 180°C/160°C Fan/Gas Mark 4. Grease a 20cm square tin with a little butter and line with baking parchment. If your banana chips are very large, roughly chop them into smaller chunks.

2 Put the butter and sugar into a large bowl and beat together for a few minutes, ideally with a handheld electric whisk, until pale and fluffy.

3 Beat in the eggs, a little at a time, until well combined. Add the Nutella and beat again briefly to combine. Sift in the flour, cocoa powder and salt, and use a spatula or large metal spoon to gently fold in. Stir through the banana chips. Transfer the batter to the prepared tin. Bake for 25–30 minutes until set on top, but still a little wobbly in the centre. Leave to cool completely.

4 To make the cereal crunch topping, put the milk chocolate, butter and golden syrup in a medium saucepan over a low heat and melt together, stirring occasionally, until combined. Pour in the cereals and stir until thoroughly coated.

5 Spoon the cereal mixture on top of the cooled brownie, using the back of a spoon to create an even layer. Press down very firmly; don't worry if you smash up the cereal up a little, you're trying to make sure this layer sticks to the brownie. Chill in the fridge for 2–3 hours, until set.

* It also means you definitely won't forget to clean your teeth afterwards.

lonesome tonight brownies

oreos, peanut butter, all the feels

A recipe for blue days, when you're feeling alone and heartbroken and wish the sofa would swallow you whole.* Such days call for a raid on the most comforting things in the cupboard; chocolate, Oreos and a big jar of peanut butter. This recipe combines all of those indulgences. Serve with Elvis's saddest tunes and a bit of a cry, but ring your mum or your best friend for a chat afterwards.

for the peanut butter batter
150g crunchy peanut butter
100g caster sugar
1 large egg

for the brownie
200g unsalted butter, chopped into rough cubes, plus extra for greasing
250g dark chocolate (around 70% cocoa solids), roughly broken into pieces
250g caster sugar
3 large eggs
140g plain flour
½ teaspoon salt
9 Oreos

1   Preheat the oven to 180°C/160°C Fan/Gas Mark 4. Grease a 20cm square tin with a little butter and line with baking parchment.

2   Make the peanut butter batter by whisking the peanut butter, sugar and egg together in a bowl until combined. Put to one side.

3   Put the butter and chocolate in a medium saucepan over a low heat and melt together, stirring frequently, until combined. Leave to cool for 5 minutes or so, until warm to the touch rather than scalding hot.

4   Gently whisk the sugar and eggs together in a bowl, just to combine, then add to the butter and chocolate pan and mix in.

5   Sift over the flour and salt, and fold in gently until combined. Transfer about half the mixture to your prepared tin. Use a teaspoon to dollop over the peanut butter batter. Add the rest of the chocolate batter, spooning it in the spaces between the peanut butter, then use a knife or skewer to swirl the peanut and chocolate batters together. Arrange the Oreos on top.

6   Bake for around 50–55 minutes. Let it cool; as these are rather gooey, it's best to put in the fridge for a few hours before slicing and devouring (if you've got the emotional strength).

*   It's cosy down there and there's usually a few buried sweets and a lost pound coin or two to cheer you up.

'help, I've got a hangover' brownies
maple syrup, crunchy bacon

One for the morning after the night before.

Salty bacon and sweet maple syrup join forces with a chewy brownie to gently tug you into the land of the living. Extra brownie points if you have the foresight to make this before you go to the pub.

for the brownie
100g smoked bacon lardons
40g maple or golden syrup
50g unsalted butter,
    chopped into rough cubes,
    plus extra for greasing
100ml vegetable oil
250g caster sugar
2 large eggs and 1 large egg
    yolk, lightly beaten
½ teaspoon vanilla paste
    or extract
80g cocoa powder
60g plain flour
50g milk chocolate, chopped
    into small chunks

for the maple glaze
(optional)
100g unsalted butter
60ml maple syrup
pinch of salt
200g icing sugar

1 Preheat the oven to 180°C/160°C Fan/Gas Mark 4. Grease a 20cm square tin with a little butter and line with baking parchment.

2 Chop the lardons into smaller pieces and add to a frying pan over a medium-high heat (there's no need for oil). Fry until crispy and golden. Add the maple syrup and cook, stirring, for a minute or 2 more, until the bacon pieces are sticky and coated. Scrape the whole lot into a bowl, including any syrup left in the pan.

3 Melt the butter in a medium saucepan over a low heat. Remove from the heat and stir in the oil and then the sugar. Add the eggs and vanilla extract and mix well to combine.

4 Sift in the cocoa powder and flour, and fold in firmly to combine – don't worry about overmixing. Stir through the bacon, plus any juices from the bacon bowl, and the milk chocolate chunks.

5 Transfer the mixture to the lined tin – it will be thick. Bake for 30–35 minutes, until set on top. Let it cool completely in the tin.

6 To make the maple glaze, melt the butter in either a microwave or a small saucepan over a low heat. Transfer to a mixing bowl and stir in the maple syrup and a pinch of salt. Sift in the icing sugar, and whisk until you have a thick, smooth glaze. Use a spoon to drizzle over the brownies. Have a Bloody Mary and some painkillers while the icing sets.

all grown-up brownies

raisins, px, almonds

Flavoured with sherry-soaked raisins and toasted almonds, this sophisticated brownie is for those days when you smugly feel like you've got adult life down (perhaps when you a land a new job, exchange contracts on your first house, or finally get to the bottom of the laundry bin).* It tastes a bit like a posh version of Cadbury's Milk Fruit & Nut. If you've not come across it before, Pedro Ximénez or 'PX' is an intensely sweet, dark sherry. It's delicious as a drink, but also fantastic in desserts. I like to serve this brownie still slightly warm, with a scoop of ice cream and an extra splosh of sherry on top.

100g raisins
4 tablespoons Pedro
    Ximénez sherry, plus extra
    to serve
100g whole blanched
    almonds
200g unsalted butter,
    chopped into rough cubes,
    plus extra for greasing
200g dark chocolate
    (around 70% cocoa solids),
    roughly broken into pieces
300g caster sugar
3 large eggs
80g plain flour
40g cocoa powder
½ teaspoon salt

1   The day before you want to make these brownies, put the raisins in a bowl with the sherry, cover and leave to soak. If you are not quite enough of an organised adult yet to make this happen, put the raisins and sherry in a small saucepan and gently simmer, stirring occasionally, until the fruit absorbs the liquid.

2   Preheat the oven to 180°C/160°C Fan/Gas Mark 4. Grease a 20cm square tin with a little butter and line with baking parchment.

3   Put the almonds in a dry frying pan over a medium heat and cook, stirring, until toasted and nicely golden (about 4–5 minutes). Tip into a bowl and put to one side to cool slightly, then roughly chop.

4   Put the butter and chocolate in a medium saucepan over a low heat, stirring frequently, until melted. Stir in the sugar, then take off the heat. Leave to cool for 5–10 minutes, until warm to the touch rather than hot.

5   Add the eggs to the pan and quickly stir to combine. Now beat, ideally using a handheld electric whisk on a medium speed, for about 3 minutes until the mixture is glossy and velvety.

6 Sift over the flour, cocoa powder and salt, and gently fold to combine. Add the raisins, plus any liquid from the bowl or saucepan (there shouldn't be more than about 1 teaspoon), plus the almonds, and stir in.

7 Transfer the mixture to your prepared tin – it will be thick – making sure to spread it to the edges. Bake for 30–35 minutes, depending on whether you want very gooey brownies or a little firmer (35 is usually perfect for me). The brownie should be set on top, with a few cracks around the edges. Let it cool in the tin for at least 30 minutes before cutting into squares and serving while it's still a little warm and gooey, with a little extra splosh of sherry.

* This is usually quite a short-lived feeling, so it's worth celebrating.

'do you like piña coladas?' blondies

toasted coconut, pineapple, rum

A taste of sunshine, with a 'holiday-sized' kick of rum. Eat and imagine you're somewhere much nicer, where the sand is as milky as white chocolate, and the two-for-one beachside cocktails are the same luminescent blue as the sea.

This is a shallow, bite-sized blondie, which has the added advantage that it can be made quickly. You can skip toasting the coconut if you're short on time, but it does intensify the flavour. I like these with a dollop of coconut cream, and ideally one of those kitsch paper umbrellas.

50g desiccated coconut, plus extra to serve if liked
120g coconut oil or unsalted butter, cut into rough cubes, plus extra for greasing
200g light brown soft sugar
1 large egg, lightly beaten
3 tablespoons rum (I use golden)
120g plain flour
¼ teaspoon salt
100g dried pineapple chunks, plus extra to serve if liked

1   Preheat the oven to 180°C/160°C Fan/Gas Mark 4. Grease a 20cm square tin with a little coconut oil or butter and line with baking parchment.

2   Put the coconut in a dry frying pan over a medium heat, and cook, stirring frequently, until it turns golden (at least 2–3 minutes). Put to one side.

3   Melt the coconut oil or butter in a medium saucepan over a low heat. Stir in the sugar, take off the heat, and leave to cool for 5 minutes.

4   Add the egg and the rum, and mix well to combine. Sift in the flour and salt, and fold in gently. Stir in the pineapple chunks and the toasted coconut, and transfer to the tin (it will be thick).

5   Bake for 22–28 minutes (depending on how gooey you like your blondies), until set on top. Let it cool, then scatter over extra coconut and pineapple chunks if liked.

gin o'clock blondies

lime, gin, juniper

A restorative glass of Mother's Ruin for elevenses may not be considered appropriate in most circles, but you can usually get away with a gin-inspired sweet treat.

Juniper berries are the key botanical used in gin; just a teaspoon gives bakes that aromatic, almost spicy G&T flavour. This blondie is more cakey than fudgy, which means you can drizzle it liberally with icing without the blondie collapsing in a drunken heap.

for the blondie
200g white chocolate, chopped into small chunks
100g unsalted butter, chopped into rough cubes, plus extra for greasing
170g light brown soft sugar
2 large eggs and 1 large egg yolk, lightly beaten
100g flour
¼ teaspoon salt
1 teaspoon juniper berries, crushed with a pestle and mortar
zest of 2 limes

for the icing
100g icing sugar
1 tablespoon lime juice
1–2 tablespoons gin

to decorate
extra lime zest or slices, if liked
paper straws

1 Preheat the oven to 180°C/160°C Fan/Gas Mark 4. Grease a 20cm square tin with a little butter and line with baking parchment.

2 Melt 100g of the white chocolate in a heatproof bowl suspended over a pan of barely simmering water (alternatively, microwave in 20-second blasts, stirring in-between, until melted). Put aside to cool slightly.

3 Put the butter and sugar in a large bowl, and cream together for a few minutes, ideally using a handheld electric mixer, until light and fluffy. Beat in the eggs a little at a time. Briefly beat in the cooled white chocolate, then sift in the flour and the salt. Add the juniper and the lime zest, then use a spatula or large metal spoon to gently bring everything together into a smooth mixture. Stir through the remaining 100g of white chocolate.

4 Transfer the mixture to the tin. Bake until set on top and golden – around 25 minutes. Leave to cool in the tin.

5 Once the blondies are cool, make the icing. Put the icing sugar in a bowl and add the lime juice and 1 tablespoon of the gin to begin with, stirring until you have a thick but drizzle-able consistency. Add the extra gin, a trickle at a time, if needed. Use a teaspoon to drizzle over the blondies. Garnish with extra lime zest or lime slices, if liked, and the straws.

when life gives you lemons blondies
lemon curd, meringue

It's hard to be grumpy when faced with a citrus fruit. Like fairy lights or small children asking dumb questions, they're too cheerful and bright not to lift your spirits. A few years ago, there was a trend for eating an orange in the shower; apparently, the intense smell and freedom from worrying about mess is a bona fide, if peculiar, cheerer-upper. I prefer to get my citrus fix in this sweet (though probably just as messy) blondie. Inspired by lemon meringue pie, it's best served straight from the oven, as an indulgent dessert.

for the blondie
160g unsalted butter,
    chopped into rough cubes,
    plus extra for greasing
130 golden caster sugar
90g light brown soft sugar
2 large eggs, lightly beaten
200g plain flour
½ teaspoon baking powder
½ teaspoon salt
100g white chocolate,
    chopped into small chunks
zest of 1 lemon, plus
    1 tablespoon juice
100g lemon curd

for the meringue topping
2 large egg whites
1 teaspoon cornflour
100g caster sugar

1   Preheat the oven to 180°C/160°C Fan/Gas Mark 4. Grease and line a 20cm square tin with baking parchment.

2   Melt the butter in a medium saucepan over a low heat. Take off the heat and let it cool for 5 minutes or so, until only just warm. Add both the sugars and stir to combine, followed by the eggs. Sift over the flour, baking powder and salt, and gently fold together until just combined. Stir in the chocolate, lemon zest and the lemon juice.

3   Transfer ⅔ of the batter to the tin and spread evenly, making sure you reach the edges; it will be quite thick, but persevere. Give the lemon curd a stir to loosen if it's very thick, then use a teaspoon to evenly dollop over the blondie batter (I usually aim for about nine dollops in a grid). Add the rest of the blondie batter to cover the curd, and smooth with the back of a spoon or knife. Bake for 25–30 minutes, depending on how cakey you want them, until set on top. Leave it to cool completely in the tin.

4   Shortly before you want to serve, make the meringue topping. Put the egg whites in a large clean bowl and whisk with a handheld electric whisk, starting slowly then increasing to a high speed, until stiff. Whisk in the cornflour briefly. Add the sugar, a spoonful at a time, as you continue whisking, until you have a stiff and glossy mixture. Spoon or pipe on top of the cooled blondies, then put under a hot grill for a few minutes or use a blowtorch, until the meringue just turns golden-brown. Eat straight away.

emergency brownie

brownie for one, in a mug

Grab a mug and set destination to the microwave. This is guaranteed to deliver an intense chocolatey hit in two minutes flat, using only store cupboard items.

Make sure to use a microwave mug without any metallic decorations, like a gold or silver trim, as this will spark an emergency of a different variety.

3 tablespoons self-raising flour
2½ tablespoons caster sugar
1½ tablespoons cocoa powder
1 tablespoon melted butter or vegetable oil
4 tablespoons milk (ideally whole)
handful of milk chocolate chips

1   Put all the ingredients in a large mug, except the chocolate chips. Stir together until you have something resembling a batter, making sure to scrape down the sides of the mug. Stir in the chocolate chips.

2   Microwave until set on top – this usually takes between 1 minute and 1 minute 30 seconds. (Microwaves vary in power, so it's best to cook this for 1 minute, check, then blast again in 30-second increments if needed.) Enjoy in pyjamas on the sofa, perhaps with a scoop of ice cream on top.

dreaming of scotland brownies

shortbread, fudge, whisky

I invented this brownie late one night, after a phone call with my parents and sisters seamlessly moved from discussions about what everyone was having for dinner to us spontaneously booking a Scottish holiday. We've spent a lot of time there in recent years. There is something about the Scottish countryside that makes me feel very peaceful – I think it's because it's the only place I go where I can't see a single flickering sign of human life, be it people or buildings, for miles around. It also helps that I really like whisky, shortbread and fudge.*

This is quite a cakey brownie, flavoured with my favourite Scottish ingredients, and is good with a cup of tea in the late afternoon. Any whisky will work, but I prefer a gentle variety, rather than a peaty Scotch.

for the shortbread base

150g unsalted butter, softened
80g golden caster sugar
230g plain flour
pinch of salt

for the brownies

120g unsalted butter, chopped into rough cubes, plus extra for greasing
150g dark chocolate (around 70% cocoa solids), roughly broken into pieces
200g golden caster sugar
2 large eggs, lightly beaten
50ml whisky
110g plain flour
¼ teaspoon sea salt, plus extra to serve if liked
100g fudge, chopped into 1cm chunks

1 Preheat the oven to 180°C/160°C/Gas Mark 4. Grease a 20cm square tin with a little butter and line with baking parchment.

2 To make the shortbread base, put the butter and sugar into a large mixing bowl and beat with a spoon to combine into a smooth paste. Add the flour and a pinch of salt, and stir to combine as much as possible, then use your hands to bring together into a rough dough. Try not to overwork it. Press the dough into the base of the tin, until you have an even layer. Prick with a fork a few times and bake for 30 minutes, until just starting to turn golden.

3 While the shortbread is in the oven, start the brownies. Put the butter and chocolate in a medium saucepan over a low heat, stirring regularly, until melted together. Take off the heat, stir in the sugar, and set aside for 10 minutes.

4 When the shortbread comes out of the oven, add the eggs to the chocolate mixture and stir to combine. Stir

in the whisky, then sift in the flour and salt, and gently fold in. Mix in the fudge pieces. Scrape the brownie mixture onto the shortbread base, smoothing to make an even layer.

5 Bake for 20–25 minutes, until set on top and a skewer comes out with just a few moist crumbs. The fudge might have made some sticky splodges on top, but don't worry. Let it cool completely in the tin, then slice and scatter over a little sea salt to serve, if liked. These are best eaten on same day.

* And Highland cows, but they don't belong in this book.

'I don't fancy cooking' brownies
dates, oats, almonds

There are times when turning the oven on seems like too much work. That's OK, and you still deserve brownies. This no-bake treat uses whizzed-up dates and nutty grounds almonds to create a convincingly squidgy texture, with minimum effort. You might notice the recipe shares some similarities with the healthy 'raw brownies' that have become popular in recent years, but with added butter and golden syrup. Sorry – my hand slipped.

400g pitted dates*
90g unsalted butter,
   chopped into rough cubes,
   plus extra for greasing
200g rolled porridge oats
200g ground almonds
180g golden or maple syrup
80g cocoa powder, plus
   extra to serve
3 tablespoons vanilla paste
   or extract
¾ teaspoon salt

1   Put the dates in a bowl and cover with just-boiled water. Leave for 10 minutes or so to soften. Meanwhile, grease and line a 20cm square tin with a little butter and line with baking parchment. Melt the butter in the microwave or in a small saucepan over a low heat.

2   Remove the dates from the bowl, reserving the water. Put them in a food processor along with the melted butter and all the other ingredients. Blitz together to make a thick paste. You want a little bit of texture, so don't whizz too much. If the mixture won't come together, add a splash of the reserved date water, but it's meant to be very thick.

3   Scrape the mixture into your lined tin and press down into a firm, even layer, using your hands or the back of a wet spoon. Refrigerate for at least 3 hours until firm. Cut into squares (this is easiest done with a knife that has been held under hot water). Sift over a little extra cocoa powder to serve.

*   Plump medjool, 'the king of dates', are particularly delicious here, but cost roughly the same as a fortnight in the Maldives, so just use the best-quality you can afford.

midnight brownies

chocolate custard, black cocoa, nibs

This is a brownie for those who love their chocolate dark; a seductive, witchy concoction to be devoured in a silky scarlet dressing gown in the middle of the night.

The base has noble heritage, descending from Nigel Slater's classic brownie – in itself a quite magical recipe, as it manages to somehow walk the tightrope between fudgy and cakey. I've also taken inspiration from Brooklyn Blackout Cake, an intensely chocolatey American classic, by adding a rich chocolate custard (who needs icing when you can have custard?). Plus cocoa nibs, for bursts of bittersweet crunch.

Black cocoa is hard to get hold of in the UK (though it can be found online) – if you manage to conjure some up, it will add an amazingly dark colour to these brownies. Otherwise, just replace with the same amount of regular cocoa.

For the dark chocolate custard

200g caster sugar
400ml whole milk
100g dark chocolate (85% cocoa solids), roughly chopped
40g cornflour
1 tablespoon golden syrup
pinch of salt
1 teaspoon vanilla paste or essence

For the brownie

160g dark chocolate (around 70% cocoa solids), finely chopped
240g caster sugar
200g unsalted butter, softened, plus extra for greasing

1 Start by making the custard. Combine all the ingredients, except the vanilla paste or essence, in a large saucepan over a medium heat. Cook gently, whisking constantly, until all the chocolate has melted and the mixture comes to the boil. Let it bubble for a few more minutes, still whisking all the time, until you have a thick, smooth, luscious custard. Stir in the vanilla, then scrape into a large, shallow dish. Cover with clingfilm, making sure you press the clingfilm onto the surface (this stops a skin forming). Put into the fridge for at least a few hours, so the custard thickens and sets.

2 Now make the brownies. Preheat the oven to 180°C/160°C Fan/Gas Mark 4. Grease a 20cm square tin with a little butter and line with greaseproof paper.

3 Put the chocolate in a heatproof bowl suspended over a pan of barely simmering water, and stir until melted (alternatively, microwave in 20-second blasts, stirring in-between, until melted). Put to one side to cool.

3 large eggs, lightly beaten
60g plain flour
20g cocoa powder
20g black cocoa powder
(or use more regular
cocoa powder)
scant ½ teaspoon baking
powder
¼ teaspoon salt
30g cocoa nibs, plus extra
to decorate

4 Put the sugar and butter in a large bowl and beat for 3 minutes or so with a handheld electric mixer (or wooden spoon) until the mixture is pale and fluffy.

5 Now slowly add the eggs, one splash at a time, while continuing to beat with your mixer or your wooden spoon. When the eggs are completely incorporated, scrape in the melted chocolate, and stir in with a spatula or large metal spoon. Sift in the flour, cocoa powders and baking powder, add the salt, and very gently fold in, until completely combined. Add the cocoa nibs and stir through.

6 Transfer the thick mixture to the prepared tin, spreading it to the edges and smoothing with a back of a spoon. Bake for 30 minutes; check, and if a skewer inserted into the centre comes out with very liquid batter on, or the brownie seems very wobbly, put it back in the oven for another 5 minutes. Let it cool completely (ideally for a few hours) before removing from the tin.

7 Take the custard from the fridge; it should now be very thick. Spoon liberally over the top of the brownie, then decorate with a few extra cocoa nibs if you like. Return to the fridge for an hour or so to set a little more before serving.

spoil yourself brownies

salted caramel, truffles

With a gooey caramel centre and a whole truffle in every square, I'll admit this is a slightly ridiculous concoction, but sometimes life calls for indulgence. If you can't find salted caramel, a tin of old-fashioned Carnation caramel comes to the rescue; just stir in sea salt to taste.

250g salted caramel sauce, plus extra to drizzle if liked
9 large chocolate truffles (I used Lindor)
150g unsalted butter, chopped into rough cubes, plus extra for greasing
200g dark chocolate (around 70% cocoa solids), roughly broken into pieces
250g golden caster sugar
3 large eggs, lightly beaten
100g plain flour

1 At least 2 hours before you want to make these brownies, put the caramel and truffles in the fridge.

2 Preheat the oven to 180°C/160°C Fan/Gas Mark 4. Grease a 20cm square tin with a little butter and line with baking parchment.

3 Put the butter and chocolate in a medium saucepan over a low heat, stirring now and again, until melted together. Stir in the sugar, then take off the heat. Leave to cool for 10 minutes or so, until warm to the touch rather than hot.

4 Add the eggs and mix in thoroughly. Sift over the flour and gently fold in.

5 Transfer half the mixture to the prepared tin and smooth it out to make an even layer. Use a teaspoon to evenly dollop over the caramel (you should get around 16 splodges). Add the rest of the brownie batter, so it completely covers the caramel.

6 Bake for 30–35 minutes, until set on top; a little wobble when you shake the tin is nothing to worry about. Let it cool in the tin for a few hours, then gently push the truffles into the top, in three rows of three. Divide into 9 plump squares; eat luxuriously, perhaps in a dressing gown or bubble bath.

'on a diet, still want brownies' brownies

chocolate, orange, secret ingredient

A recipe for those days when you're trying to eat more lightly, yet still crave chocolate.* I can't claim this is good for you, but it is considerably lower in chocolate, butter and sugar than your average brownie. I trialled all sorts of tricks while trying to develop a healthier brownie, from adding chickpeas to mayonnaise, but the results all tasted a little sad (and of chickpeas and mayonnaise). The best solution was butternut squash. Sweet and soft, it helps create a convincing brownie texture without interrupting the chocolate flavour. You can also use sweet potato, but squash brings a nice hint of nuttiness (it's lower in calories, too).

Chocolate orange is a classic flavour combination, but feel free to use ordinary dark chocolate and skip the orange zest if it's not to your taste.

300g peeled, deseeded butternut squash

100g dark chocolate with orange (around 70% cocoa solids), roughly broken into pieces

100g unsalted butter, chopped into rough cubes, plus extra for greasing

2 large eggs

200g golden caster sugar

2 teaspoons vanilla paste or extract

zest of 1 orange

80g plain flour

40g cocoa powder, plus extra to serve

¼ teaspoon baking powder

¼ teaspoon salt

50g milk chocolate, chopped into small chunks

---

1 Preheat the oven to 180°C/160°C Fan/Gas Mark 4. Grease a 20cm square tin with a little butter and line with baking parchment.

2 Chop the butternut squash into 2–3cm chunks. Put in a bowl with 2 tablespoons of water, cover and microwave for around 5–8 minutes until the squash is completely cooked through and tender (the time will vary depending on your microwave). Drain any remaining water from the bowl and either whizz the squash in a food processor or mash thoroughly with a fork until you have a smooth purée. You should have between 230g and 250g. Leave aside to cool.

3 Put the dark chocolate and the butter in a saucepan over a low heat, stirring frequently until melted together. Take off the heat and mix in the squash purée. Let it cool for 5 minutes.

4 Put the eggs in a bowl with the sugar and gently whisk for a few seconds, to combine. Add to the saucepan, along with the vanilla paste or extract and orange zest,

and mix to combine. Sift in the flour, cocoa powder, baking powder and salt, and gently fold together. Stir through the milk chocolate chunks.

5 Transfer the batter to the tin. Bake for 20–25 minutes; the brownie shouldn't have any movement when you shake the tin and it should feel firm and springy to the touch.

* So ... most days.

the journey of chocolate

Sweet yet bitter, creamy yet dark, chocolate's complex flavour has sent our senses into overdrive for thousands of years. The Mayans and Aztecs revered chocolate as a gift from the gods, believing it endowed them with strength and health. In the seventeenth century, gossiping Londoners gobbled up pamphlets that claimed chocolate was an aphrodisiac, able to make men as 'nimble as a squirrel [sic]'* in the bedroom.

What makes chocolate so irresistible remains a little bit of a mystery. Its chemical compounds certainly trigger the 'pleasure centres' of our brain, lighting it up like a Christmas tree. But there are other factors at play, too. Some scientists argue that milk chocolate's fat-to-sugar ratio is very similar to that of breast milk (apologies if that makes you choke on your bar of Cadbury's). In her book *Cocoa*, food writer Sue Quinn points out that chocolate is the only food that melts at around body temperature; the sensation of rich, smooth chocolate flooding the mouth is something our brains, if not our dentists, find uniquely pleasing.

Whatever the reason, more than seven million tons of chocolate treats, from airport Toblerones to vending machine KitKats, are now scoffed around the world every year. A complicated network of technology, trade and transport exists to feed this global appetite – but every cup, bar or bite of chocolate begins, as it always has, with a tropical tree.

harvesting

The *Theobroma* cacao tree probably originated in the dense forests of the Amazon, though it now grows in hot and humid countries across the world, from Indonesia to Nigeria. Around twice a year, farmers gently harvest its rugby ball-sized pods by hand, then split them open to reveal the prize – up to 60 cacao beans inside each one, cushioned like jewels in a fibrous white pulp.

fermenting

The beans are carefully scooped out, put in boxes, bags or on a bed of banana leaves, then covered and left to ferment for up to 8 days. The farmers turn them once or twice to introduce more oxygen. Slowly, the beans darken, lose their astringency and develop some of those deep, rich

* The most famously virile of animals.

flavours we recognise as chocolate; though at this point, you still wouldn't enjoy eating one.

drying and roasting
The fermented beans are dried, traditionally by putting them in the open air for a sunbathe. They are then sent to chocolate makers, who roast them to develop the flavour even further. Roasting has a big impact on the chocolate's final taste; the exact time and temperature is often a closely-guarded secret of the manufacturer.

grinding and 'conching'
The beans' shells are removed, leaving behind the 'nibs', which are ground to create a thick paste know as cacao mass or liquor. Other ingredients are added, depending on the type of chocolate being made – such as sugar, milk solids or powder, cocoa butter or vanilla. The chocolate maker will grind, mix and refine the paste even more, according to their preferred methods, and the texture and mouthfeel they are aiming for. Part of this process is traditionally done in a machine poetically called a 'conch', so named because the original machine looked like a shell.

tempering
The chocolate is finished by a process known as 'tempering' – bringing liquid chocolate slowly to a certain temperature before allowing it to cool and solidify. This is what gives chocolate its shiny surface and characteristic 'snap'. The journey of chocolate, from bitter bean to crowd-pleasing bar, is complete.

a note on provenance

Chocolate making may sound like a smooth process, but it's not always a sweet one. Exploitation has been an ingredient in the global chocolate business since its very beginnings. Like sugar and coffee, cocoa was once picked and processed by African slaves, who laboured in grim conditions so rich Europeans could show off the fashionable foodstuff at dinner parties. Today, many cacao farmers earn well under a living wage, while child labour, trafficking and deforestation are also serious concerns. Given the complexity and opacity of the chocolate supply chain, it can be hard for consumers to discover the truth behind their bars, but try and seek out ethically-minded brands with clear principles to make your brownies with. It will leave a better taste.

brownies for celebration

'I think I love you' brownies

red velvet, raspberries, cheesecake

A little love poem in brownie form for the newly besotted. Or, if you're in a relationship, a way to make up with your partner after fighting over whose turn it is to take the bin out.*

You need good-quality food colouring to give the batter that authentic red velvet shade; look for a gel or paste from a cake decorating shop or website, rather than those little bottles of liquid in the supermarket.

for the cheesecake
150g full-fat cream cheese
1 large egg yolk (save the
    white for the brownie)
2 tablespoons caster sugar
1 tablespoon plain flour
½ teaspoon vanilla paste
    or extract

for the brownie
110g unsalted butter,
    chopped into rough cubes,
    plus extra for greasing
150g dark chocolate (around
    70% cocoa solids), roughly
    broken into pieces
190g caster sugar
2 large eggs and 1 large egg
    white, lightly beaten
½–1 teaspoon concentrated
    red food colouring gel
    or paste
80g plain flour
¼ teaspoon salt
¼ teaspoon baking powder
150g raspberries

1   Preheat the oven to 180°C/160°C Fan/Gas Mark 4. Grease a 20cm square tin with a little butter and line with baking parchment.

2   To make the cheesecake mixture, put all the ingredients in a bowl and gently whisk together until smooth (don't overmix, or it will go runny). Pop in the fridge briefly while you make the brownie.

3   Put the butter and chocolate in a medium saucepan over a low heat, stirring frequently, until melted together. Take off the heat and leave to cool for 5–10 minutes.

4   Stir in the sugar, then stir in the eggs and ½ teaspoon of the food colouring. Sift over the flour, salt and baking powder, and fold in. You can add more food colouring at this stage if the mixture doesn't look very red. Stir through two-thirds of the raspberries and transfer to the lined tin, making sure to spread it to the edges.

5   Use a teaspoon to dollop the cheesecake mix over the brownie batter, and use a skewer or the tip of a knife to swirl together gently. Carefully place the remaining raspberries lightly around the cheesecake swirl. Bake for 35–40 minutes; cover with foil after 25–30 minutes to stop the cheesecake colouring too much. Let it cool before giving to the lucky recipient.

* It is always their turn to take the bin out.

after-dinner brownies

mint chocolate, a taste of adulthood

When I was small, the after-dinner mint felt like a gateway into the glamorous, secret world of grown-ups. After Eights, each one tucked away like a gift in its individual glossy, rustling sleeve, were the most inviting; I would sneak them from my parents' table whenever I got the chance. I still can't resist the combination of mint and chocolate in any form, whether it's toothpaste-flavoured ice cream or a lurid green cocktail.

This brownie is what I make when people are coming round for dinner, and a proper pudding seems too formal. You can make it with any mint chocolate, but something like Aero, with its bubbly green interior, looks most effective. Serve small squares straight from the fridge, along with coffee, and don't invite anyone back who claims not to like mint chocolate. They clearly still have some growing up to do.

200g mint Aero chocolate or similar (plus extra for decorating the top, if liked)

200g unsalted butter, chopped into rough cubes, plus extra for greasing

250g dark chocolate (around 70% cocoa solids), roughly broken into pieces

250g caster sugar

3 large eggs

½–1 teaspoon peppermint essence

80g plain flour

40g cocoa powder

½ teaspoon salt

1 Preheat the oven to 180°C/160°C Fan/Gas Mark 4. Grease a 20cm square tin with a little butter and line with baking parchment. Break or chop the Aero into unevenly-sized chunks; I like to make mine quite big, around 3cm. Leave to one side.

2 Put the butter and chocolate in a medium saucepan over a low heat, stirring regularly, until melted then take off the heat. Stir in the sugar, and leave to cool until only just warm – this is important, or I am afraid your mint chocolate chunks will melt in an unappetising, Shrek-coloured mess.

3 Add the eggs and stir in the peppermint essence. (Essences vary in strength, so start with the smaller amount if you have a strong one, or if you don't want too intense a minty flavour.)

4 Beat using a handheld electric whisk, on a medium speed, for about 2 minutes, until smoother and a little thicker (you can use a normal balloon whisk if you prefer, but give it another minute or so).

5 Sift in the flour, cocoa powder and salt, and fold gently to combine. Taste, and add a little more peppermint essence if you like. Mix in two-thirds of the Aero chunks, keeping back a third to press on top. Transfer to your prepared tin, getting it right to the edges, and scatter the remaining Aero chunks on top, pressing in very gently with your fingers. I usually angle the chunks on their side, so you can see the green interior.

6 Bake for 25–30 minutes, until set on top. Let it cool completely before slicing. I like these best when served straight from the fridge.

falling into autumn brownies
blackberries, rye, bay

Autumn is my favourite time of year. As summer packs its bags, I eagerly look out for those first signs of the new season: cosy jumpers barging flimsy bikinis out of shop windows; carpets of golden leaves that need to be swept off car roofs in the morning; and, best of all, the blackberries that swell up on the hedgerows like inky balloons, ready to be popped into jams, crumbles and brownies.

Here, I've combined blackberries with nutty rye flour and studded the top with a drift of bay leaves. The idea of putting bay leaves on brownies comes from the West Country cook Gill Meller; although it sounds a little strange, they infuse the brownies with a woody, slightly savoury quality, which offsets the sweetness. These smell like autumn when you take them out of the oven.

170g unsalted butter, chopped into rough cubes, plus extra for greasing
150g dark chocolate (around 70% cocoa solids), roughly broken into pieces
100g milk chocolate, roughly broken into pieces
150g golden caster sugar
100 light muscovado sugar
3 large eggs
120g rye flour
¼ teaspoon salt
150g blackberries
6–8 bay leaves (fresh is best)

1 Preheat the oven to 180°C/160°C Fan/Gas Mark 4. Grease a 20cm square tin with a little butter and line with baking parchment.

2 Melt the butter and chocolates in a medium saucepan on a low heat, stirring, until melted. Take off the heat and stir in the sugars. Leave to cool for 5 minutes or so.

3 Add the eggs to the pan and quickly stir to combine. Now beat, ideally using a handheld electric whisk on a medium speed, for about 3 minutes until thick and glossy.

4 Sift over the flour and salt, and gently fold in until just combined. Transfer half the batter to your prepared tin, making sure to spread to the edges. Scatter over two-thirds of the blackberries. Spread over the rest of the batter. Scatter the remaining blackberries over the top, and arrange the bay leaves around them.

5 Bake for around 40–45 minutes. The brownie should be set on top, with a few cracks, and there shouldn't be much movement at all when you shake the tin. These are best refrigerated before serving.

'thank god it's payday' brownies

caramel, shortbread chunks, all that glitters

A glitzy number to celebrate the top-up of your bank account. These are inspired by the retro bakery treat millionaire's shortbread, and will vanish quicker than your pay cheque.

for the brownie layer

100g shortbread
200g unsalted butter, chopped into rough cubes, plus extra for greasing
200g dark chocolate (around 70% cocoa solids), chopped into rough chunks
150g golden caster sugar
100g light brown soft sugar
3 large eggs, lightly beaten
140g plain flour
¼ teaspoon salt

for the caramel

70g unsalted butter
1 x 379g tin sweetened condensed milk
50g golden syrup
50g light brown soft sugar

for the chocolate topping

200g dark or milk chocolate, roughly chopped
1 tablespoon golden syrup
edible gold leaf, gold glitter spray or gold chocolate coins to decorate (optional)

1   Preheat the oven to 180°C/160°C Fan/Gas Mark 4. Grease a 20cm square tin with a little butter and line with baking parchment.

2   Chop 80g of the shortbread into small chunks. Put the rest to one side.

3   Put the butter and chocolate in a medium saucepan over a low heat, stirring regularly, until melted together. Take off the heat. Stir in the sugars, and leave to cool for 5 minutes.

4   Add the eggs and mix until well combined. Sift in the flour and salt, and fold in gently. Stir through the shortbread chunks then transfer to the tin.

5   Bake for 30–35 minutes, until the brownie is set, with a few cracks at the edges and little to no movement in the centre. Let it cool for a few hours.

6   To make the caramel layer, put all the ingredients into a saucepan and place on a low heat. Keep stirring until the sugar has dissolved and the butter has melted, then turn up the heat and bubble fairly vigorously for about 5–10 minutes. Make sure you stir the mixture constantly, or it will catch and burn on the bottom of the pan. The caramel is ready when it turns a golden caramel colour and has thickened slightly. Take off the heat and let it cool for 5 minutes. Pour over the brownie carefully – it will be very hot – and spread out evenly using a spatula

or spoon. Leave to cool; I usually put it in the fridge for at least 30 minutes.

7   To make the topping, melt the chocolate with the golden syrup in the microwave or in a heatproof bowl over a pan of simmering water. Pour over the caramel. Crumble the remaining 20g of shortbread with your fingers and scatter over the chocolate. Leave to set, ideally in the fridge, for an hour or 2 before serving.

8   For the full millionaire's treatment, decorate with chocolate coins, edible gold leaf or gold glitter spray before serving.

happy easter brownies
vanilla fudge, chocolate eggs

Easter is the best holiday celebration; it offers all the feel-good togetherness of Christmas, with less stress and more chocolate. This is a triple threat brownie worthy of the event: a luscious chocolate base crowned with a layer of chocolatey fudge, finished with a scattering of chocolate eggs. It's rich, so serve in small squares.

for the brownie
120g unsalted butter, chopped into rough cubes, plus extra for greasing
150g dark chocolate (around 70% cocoa solids), roughly broken into pieces
200g caster sugar
2 large eggs, lightly beaten
2 tablespoons whole or semi-skimmed milk
100g plain flour
¼ teaspoon salt

for the vanilla fudge topping
1 x 397 tin condensed milk
200g dark chocolate (at least 50% cocoa solids), roughly broken into pieces
100g milk chocolate, roughly broken into pieces
30g icing sugar
2 teaspoons vanilla paste or extract

to decorate
whole chocolate eggs, broken up (a mix of sizes looks good)
80g multicoloured mini chocolate eggs

1 Preheat the oven to 180°C/160°C Fan/Gas Mark 4. Grease a 20cm square tin with a little butter and line with baking parchment.

2 Melt the butter and chocolate gently together in a medium saucepan over a low heat, stirring regularly. Stir in the sugar, take off the heat and set aside for 5 minutes or so, until a little cooler.

3 Add the eggs and mix in well. Stir in the milk, then sift over the flour and salt, and gently fold to combine. Scrape the brownie mixture into the prepared tin and smooth to the edges. Bake for 20–25 minutes, until set on top and there's very little movement in the pan. Leave to cool.

4 To make the fudge topping, put the condensed milk and both chocolates in a saucepan over a very low heat, stirring frequently, until melted together. Take off the heat and stir in the icing sugar and vanilla. Spread over the cooled brownie; it will be very thick.

5 Check the temperature of the fudge topping by holding a finger lightly against it – by this point it should feel only just warm. Decorate with the shards of broken egg and mini eggs, very gently pushing them into the fudge. (If the topping still feels hot, let it cool briefly before adding the eggs.) Chill in the fridge for 2–3 hours, until the fudge has set.

afternoon tea blondies
scones and jam

What goes first on a scone, cream or jam? Who cares? Avoid the whole tedious discussion by making this blondie instead.

100g–120g strawberry or raspberry jam
160g unsalted butter, chopped into rough cubes, plus extra for greasing
240g light brown soft sugar
2 large eggs, lightly beaten
1 teaspoon vanilla paste or extract
220g plain flour
½ teaspoon baking powder
¼ teaspoon salt
100g white chocolate, chopped into small chunks
1 small scone

1 Preheat the oven to 180°C/160°C Fan/Gas Mark 4. Grease a 20cm square tin with a little butter and line with baking parchment. Put the jam into a bowl and loosen slightly by stirring with a spoon or fork.

2 Melt the butter in a large pan over a low heat. Stir in the sugar, remove from the heat and leave to cool for 5–10 minutes, until warm to the touch rather than hot.

3 Stir in the eggs and vanilla. Sift over the flour, baking powder and salt, and gently fold together. Add the white chocolate and stir through.

4 Transfer the batter to the prepared tin. Use a teaspoon to drop about 12 dollops of jam evenly on top of the blondie. Smear each dollop gently with the back of the spoon, then roughly crumble the scone into small pieces and scatter on top, ideally avoiding the splodges of jam.

5 Bake for 28–35 minutes, until set on top with only a slight wobble in the centre. Let it cool before serving, with a scoop of clotted cream and a cup of tea.

wedding bells blondies
caramelised white chocolate, summer berries, champagne cream

Many couples now ask guests to bring a homemade bake to their wedding, to add to a shared dessert table, instead of having the traditional tiered cake. These beautiful golden squares, somewhere between a blondie and a traybake, are just the thing. You can dress them up even fancier with extra fruit and edible flowers.*

Caramelising white chocolate takes a little time, but is worth it; the chocolate develops a rich, complex flavour, which is the perfect partner for the tart berries. Some relationships are meant to be.

for the blondie
200g white chocolate,
    roughly chopped
150g unsalted butter,
    chopped into rough cubes,
    plus extra for greasing
100g light brown soft sugar
100g caster sugar
2 large eggs, lightly beaten
140g plain flour
60g ground almonds
¼ teaspoon baking powder
½ teaspoon salt
100g summer fruits,
    such as raspberries,
    cherries, redcurrants
    and blueberries (avoid
    strawberries, as they
    tend to be too soggy)

for the champagne cream
300ml double cream
100ml champagne (or other
    sparkling wine)

1   First, make the caramelised white chocolate. Preheat the oven to 140°C/120°C Fan/Gas Mark 1. Spread the chopped white chocolate out evenly on a baking tray and cook for 10 minutes, then stir and smooth out the melting chocolate with a spatula. Repeat this process, stirring the chocolate every 10 minutes, until it is a deep golden colour. This can take anywhere between 30 minutes and 1 hour. At one point, the chocolate might seize up and look strange and chalky, but keep stirring and moving it, and eventually it will become smooth. Scrape 100g into a medium saucepan, and transfer the remainder into a bowl to cool down.

2   Turn up the oven 180°C/160°C Fan/Gas Mark 4. Grease a 20cm square tin with a little butter and line with baking parchment.

3   Add the butter to the saucepan containing the caramelised chocolate, and melt together, stirring frequently, over a low heat. Remove from the heat and leave to cool for 10–15 minutes.

4   Add the sugars to the butter mixture and stir to combine. Add the eggs and stir well to make a smooth batter. Sift over the flour, almonds, baking powder and salt, and fold to combine.

5 Transfer the batter to your prepared tin. Give the bowl of leftover caramelised chocolate a stir to check the consistency – you want it to be thick but drizzle-able, like caramel. If it has stiffened up too much, give it a few 10-second blasts in the microwave, stirring in-between, until it's runnier. Use a spoon to drizzle over the chocolate in 5 or 6 thick, evenly spaced stripes. Very gently drag a skewer or the tip of a knife through the stripes in the opposite direction, to create a feathered effect. Scatter over the summer fruit, but don't press into the batter.

6 Bake for around 40 minutes; the blondie should be golden brown and set on top, but still have a little wobble in the centre. Let it cool completely before cutting into squares.

7 To make the champagne cream, whip the cream to soft peaks with an electric or handheld whisk, then gradually whisk in the champagne. (You can add a spoon of icing sugar if you'd like this sweeter, but I like the contrast of the slightly tangy cream against the sweet blondie.)

8 Serve the blondies with a dollop of the cream, plus extra berries and edible flowers if you fancy. These are best eaten on the day they are made.

* This is a sure-fire way to outshine the other guests, even more effective than wearing the biggest hat.

birthday blondies

vanilla, sprinkles, whipped cream

I created these for my little sister Rebecca's 24th. It was a bit of a muted birthday because she is a nurse and it was the height of the Covid-19 crisis, so we sat at a safe distance in the garden, and ate these sprinkle-topped squares to make the best of it. The recipe is loosely based on American writer Mark Bittman's famous blondie, which is very dense, rich and sugary – but so a birthday blondie should be.

A word of caution about baking with sprinkles, from bitter sprinkle experience; the types sold in supermarkets to decorate cupcakes with are not very heat resistant and will melt away in the batter (they're just coloured sugar, after all). I buy mine from dedicated baking shops or online; the long strands known as 'jimmies' in the US work well.

for the blondie

130g unsalted butter, chopped into rough cubes, plus extra for greasing
130g light brown soft sugar
80g caster sugar
1 large egg and 1 large egg yolk, lightly beaten
1 tablespoon vanilla paste or extract
170g plain flour
¼ teaspoon salt
100g white chocolate, chopped into small
50g sprinkles (see intro)

for the whipped cream topping

200ml double cream
1 tablespoon icing sugar
1 teaspoon vanilla paste or extract
extra sprinkles, to serve

1 Preheat the oven to 180°C/160°C Fan/Gas Mark 4. Grease a 20cm square tin with a little butter and line with baking parchment.

2 Melt the butter in a medium saucepan on a low heat. Take off the heat, stir in the sugars to dissolve, and leave until only just warm – this is Very Important, or your sprinkles will melt too quickly. Stir in the eggs and vanilla, then sift in the flour and salt, and mix to combine. Stir in the chocolate chunks and sprinkles.

3 Transfer to the prepared tin. Bake for about 25 minutes, until set on top. Let it cool completely (this is also Very Important, as otherwise the topping will slide right off). Just before you're ready to serve, put the double cream, icing sugar and vanilla into a large bowl and beat with a whisk until you have soft peaks. Spoon over the blondie, and decorate with as many sprinkles as you like.

bewitching halloween brownies

pumpkin, spices, white chocolate ghosts

Brownies flavoured with warming spices and a ripple of pumpkin batter make for a much better Halloween snack than the dregs of the 'trick or treat' bowl.

The ghost decorations aren't essential but are fun to make if you've got children in the house – or someone like me, who jumps at the excuse to celebrate Halloween.

For the pumpkin batter
100g pumpkin purée, from a tin
100g full-fat cream cheese
40g caster sugar
1 large egg yolk
1 tablespoon plain flour
1½ teaspoons ground cinnamon
½ teaspoon ground ginger

for the brownie
100g unsalted butter, chopped into rough cubes, plus extra for greasing
200g dark chocolate (around 70% cocoa solids), roughly broken into pieces
3 large eggs
240g caster sugar
140g plain flour
½ teaspoon baking powder
¼ teaspoon salt

for the white chocolate ghosts (optional)
100g white chocolate, roughly chopped
black food colouring

1   Preheat the oven to 180°C/160°C Fan/Gas Mark 4. Grease a 20cm square tin with a little butter and line with baking parchment.

2   Put the ingredients for the pumpkin batter in a bowl, and gently whisk together, breaking up any lumps (don't beat too much, or the mixture will go runny). Transfer to the fridge to chill slightly while you make the brownie batter.

3   Melt the butter and chocolate together in a medium saucepan over a low heat, stirring frequently. Take off the heat and set aside at least 10 minutes to cool.

4   Whisk the eggs and sugar very lightly together in a bowl, until just combined, then add to the chocolate mixture and stir vigorously to combine.

5   Sift over the flour, baking powder and salt, and gently fold in.

6   Put half the brownie batter into the prepared tin and smooth to the edges. Using a teaspoon, dollop over half the pumpkin batter in evenly spaced blobs, then add the rest of the chocolate batter and smooth over the top. Dollop over the rest of the pumpkin batter as before. Now use a skewer or the tip of a knife to gently swirl the batters together; don't over-do it. Bake for around 40 minutes until set on top, and with only a little movement in the centre. Leave to cool.

7 While the brownies are baking, make the white chocolate ghosts. Line a baking tray with baking parchment. Put aside 20g of the white chocolate and melt the rest, either by placing in a heatproof bowl over a pan of simmering water and stirring until melted, or by microwaving in 20-second intervals, stirring in-between, until melted and smooth. Leave to cool for 5–10 minutes until thickened slightly. Dollop a teaspoon of chocolate on the prepared tray and use the back of the spoon to spread the chocolate into a ghost shape, making sure you're not spreading it too thin. Repeat, until you have 8–10 ghosts. Chill in the fridge until set, then use a paintbrush or toothpick dipped into the black food colouring to draw on eyes and mouths.

8 Gently remove the ghosts from the baking paper (a palette knife makes this easier). Melt the white chocolate you put aside earlier (following the same method as you did above), then use the melted chocolate to stick the ghosts onto the cooled brownies.

bonfire brownies

biscuit base, golden syrup, marshmallows

A brownie for Guy Fawkes Night, to hold in mittened hands as you watch fireworks shatter the sky. The flavours are inspired by the American campfire favourite, S'mores, but the hint of caramel is down to that old-fashioned British ingredient, golden syrup. Ideally use a spring-release tin, as the base can be tricky to lever out. These are easiest sliced with a knife that has been run under hot water.

for the biscuit layer

200g digestive biscuits
100g unsalted butter,
  chopped into rough cubes
2 tablespoons golden syrup
pinch of salt

for the brownie

120g dark chocolate (around
  70% cocoa solids), roughly
  broken into pieces
100g unsalted butter,
  chopped into rough cubes,
  plus extra for greasing
100g caster sugar
100g golden syrup
2 large eggs, lightly beaten
80g plain flour
½ teaspoon salt
200g large marshmallows

* Do not under any circumstances allow yourself to be distracted by washing up, small children or handsome strangers passing the window – marshmallows can burn quickly, so they need your full attention.

1 Preheat the oven to 180°C/160°C Fan/Gas Mark 4. Grease a 20cm square tin with a little butter and line with baking parchment.

2 Put the digestive biscuits in a plastic bag and crush with a rolling pin to fine crumbs. Put the butter, golden syrup and salt in a saucepan over a low heat, stirring frequently, until melted together. Take off the heat, then add the biscuits to the saucepan and mix thoroughly until the crumbs are completely coated. Tip the mixture into the prepared tin and press down into a compact, even layer. Bake for 8–10 minutes until firm.

3 For the brownie layer, put the chocolate, butter, sugar and golden syrup in a medium saucepan over a low heat. Cook, stirring, until melted together. Take off the heat and leave to cool for 5 minutes.

4 Add the eggs to the pan and stir to combine. Sift in the flour and salt, and gently fold until just combined. Spread the brownie over the biscuit base and bake for 20–25 minutes; the brownie should be set on top, with no jiggle when you shake the tin and no more than a few crumbs on the skewer. Leave to cool as long as you can (or the base will be rather crumbly).

5 Heat the grill to medium-high. Place the marshmallows on top of the brownie in a single layer, evenly spaced apart, and put under the grill until the marshmallows are collapsing and turning golden brown. This can take anywhere between 1 and 4 minutes.* Serve immediately.

'it's beginning to feel a lot like christmas' brownies

cinnamon, ginger, clementine drizzle

I love the quiet, anticipatory joyfulness of the-time-before-Christmas. My family roll their eyes when I start making pros-and-cons lists for joints of meat in October ('Could this be a goose year?'), and roll them even harder when I insist on putting up the tree on the very first day of December – but in a world full of sharp edges, I see no harm in embracing the fuzzy warmth of the festive season as soon as you can.

This is a brownie for that first day when you catch the smell of cinnamon and sugar from a bakery, or spot the perfect gift for someone in the corner of your favourite shop, and think 'Yes – Christmas is on its way'.

for the brownie

170g unsalted butter, chopped into rough cubes, plus extra for greasing
150g dark chocolate (around 70% cocoa solids), roughly broken into pieces
100g milk chocolate, roughly broken into pieces
250g golden caster sugar
3 large eggs
120g plain flour
½ teaspoon salt
2 teaspoons cinnamon
½ teaspoon nutmeg
¼ teaspoon ground cloves
80g chopped walnuts or another favourite festive nut (optional)

for the clementine drizzle

150g icing sugar
2 clementines, zest and juice

1 Preheat the oven to 180°C/160°C Fan/Gas Mark 4. Grease a 20cm square tin with a little butter and line with baking parchment. Put on your favourite Christmas album.

2 Put the butter and both types of chocolate in a saucepan over a low heat, stirring, until melted and smooth. Leave to cool for 5 minutes.

3 Put the sugar and eggs in a bowl and gently whisk until just combined, then add to the saucepan and mix in. Sift the flour, salt and spices into the pan, and gently fold together. Mix in the walnuts (or other nuts), if using.

4 Transfer the mixture to your prepared tin, getting it right to the edges. Bake for 30–35 minutes (or push to 40 if you'd like a more cakey texture). The brownie should be set on top, with a few cracks around the edges. Let it cool completely in the tin, preferably in the fridge, before cutting into Christmas tree-like triangles (though you can cut into squares if you prefer). For triangles, the easiest method is to slice the brownie horizontally into three rows, then divide each of those pieces into 5 triangles.

to decorate

silver balls, hundreds and thousands or other decorations (for the trees)

chocolate fingers, matchmakers or candy cane sticks (for the tree trunks)

5   To make the drizzle, mix the icing sugar with the zest of both clementines and enough juice to make a thick, smooth icing – I usually find the juice of 1 clementine is enough, but it depends on your fruit. Use a teaspoon to drizzle over the brownies and decorate with silver balls or other edible decorations.

6   Chop your chocolate fingers, Matchmakers or candy canes to create small tree 'trunks', and insert into the base of each triangle.

'too good for children' christmas brownies

marzipan, pear, chestnut, irish cream

A gathering of festive flavours under a boozy Irish cream frosting, this is the all-grown-up sequel to my 'It's beginning to feel a lot like Christmas' brownie on page 130. I love the slight nutty taste and soft texture imparted by the spelt flour, but you can swap for plain if you prefer.

I sometimes decorate these with extra slices of pear and a scattering of marzipan cubes.

for the brownie
100g marzipan
200g dark chocolate (around 70% cocoa solids), roughly broken into pieces
100g unsalted butter, chopped into rough cubes, plus extra for greasing
240g light brown soft sugar
3 large eggs
70g wholegrain spelt flour
50g ground almonds
1 tablespoon cocoa powder
¼ teaspoon baking powder
¼ teaspoon salt
1 pear, peeled, cored and diced

for the chestnut and Irish cream icing
100ml double cream
50g unsweetened chestnut purée
1 tablespoon icing sugar
1–2 tablespoons Irish cream (such as Baileys)

* It is important to taste the icing repeatedly to decide this.

1 About half an hour before you want to make the brownies, chop the marzipan into small chunks (about 1cm) and pop into the freezer – this stops them melting away.

2 Preheat the oven to 180°C/160°C Fan/Gas Mark 4. Grease and line a 20cm square tin with baking parchment.

3 Put the chocolate and butter in a saucepan over a low heat and melt very gently, stirring regularly. Take off the heat and leave to cool for 5 minutes.

4 Put the sugar and eggs in a large bowl and gently whisk until just combined. Add to the saucepan and mix in. Add the flour, ground almonds, cocoa powder, baking powder and salt, and fold in until just combined. Take the marzipan out of the freezer, prising apart any chunks that have stuck together, and tip into the saucepan. Add the pear chunks and stir through gently to disperse. Transfer the mixture to the prepared tin, getting into all the edges, and bake for 30–35 minutes, until set on top. Let it cool completely in the tin.

5 To make the icing, put the cream, chestnut purée and icing sugar in a large bowl and beat, ideally using a handheld electric whisk, until soft and fluffy. Add the Irish cream, a little at a time, stopping only when you're satisfied the icing has a decent Baileys kick.* If the icing seems a little runny after you've added the alcohol, beat it a little more until you reach your desired consistency. Spread the icing over the brownie and decorate as desired.

snow day brownies*

toblerone, cocoa, honeyed almonds

I came up with this recipe one cold and snowy Saturday in the middle of winter. Snow days as an adult are never quite as good as your childhood memories – probably because you don't get the day off work to build snowmen – but I still get a little tingle of excitement on those rare mornings when you wake up, and the light in your bedroom has that curious glowing quality, and you know, even before you tug open the curtains, that the view outside will be totally transformed.

I've crowned these brownies with chunky triangles of Toblerone, whose shape nods to snow-topped mountains, plus honeyed almonds to echo that delicious nougat-y Toblerone flavour. Tuck in after a bracing walk/snowball fight/sledge, and remember to dust with icing sugar for the full wintry effect.

60g flaked almonds

2 teaspoons runny honey

1 large white or milk chocolate Toblerone (360g)

150g unsalted butter, chopped into rough cubes, plus extra for greasing

240g caster sugar

2 large eggs and 1 large egg yolk, lightly beaten

80g cocoa powder

60g plain flour

icing sugar, to decorate

sea salt

1 Preheat the oven to 200°C/180°C Fan/Gas Mark 6. Scatter the nuts on a baking tray lined with baking parchment. Cook for 3 minutes, then drizzle over the honey and a sprinkling of sea salt, and stir to combine, making sure to break up any big clumps. Put back in the oven for a further 3–5 minutes until golden, then put aside to cool slightly. Roughly chop the almonds and 2 triangles of the Toblerone.

2 Turn down the oven to 180°C/160°C Fan/Gas Mark 4. Grease a 20cm square tin with a little butter and line with baking parchment.

3 Melt the butter in a medium saucepan over a low heat. Remove from the heat and stir in the sugar. Leave for 3–5 minutes to cool slightly. Add the eggs and mix well to combine.

4 Sift in the cocoa powder, flour and ¼ teaspoon of salt, and fold in firmly to combine – don't worry about overmixing. Tumble in the almonds and the chopped Toblerone, stirring to combine.

5 Transfer the mixture to the lined tin, making sure to spread to the edges – it will be quite thick. Break the remaining Toblerone into triangles and arrange 9 on top. This will leave exactly one triangle to eat as a chef's perk.

6 Bake for 30–35 minutes; they should have a faint wobble when you shake the tin, and a skewer plunged into the middle should come out gungy, but not covered in liquid. Let cool completely in the tin. Cut into squares and sift over icing sugar to serve if you like.

* An alternative name is 'I got you this at the airport' brownies – as it's unofficial policy that you're not allowed to leave an airport without buying an emergency gift of novelty-shaped Swiss chocolate. They'd also be a good gift for someone about to go skiing – or someone like me, who enjoys the culture around skiing (dinky chalets, spas, molten cheese) but doesn't have much desire to fall down a hill with everyone watching. I've got nightmares for that.

'help, my brownies are dry!' and other brownie problems

why are brownies difficult to slice?
Brownies and blondies can be harder to cut than the tension in your favourite crime drama. The very same squidginess that makes them so tasty means they're stubbornly resistant to being sliced into neat squares. My top tip is to let them cool completely before trying (hide the knives from greedy housemates if you must). For easier slicing, refrigerate them first.

what if I want to eat them now?
Use the ice bath method. Fill a large roasting pan with cold water and ice cubes, then plunge the tin of just-cooked brownies straight in. This trick not only cools the brownies down, it prevents them from continuing to cook in the tin – meaning an even gooier result. Just make sure you don't accidentally splash or submerge the brownies; water will certainly make them moist, but not in the way you want.

why are my brownies dry?
Check your oven isn't running too hot; an oven thermometer is helpful here. If the problem recurs, start checking your brownies about two-thirds of the way through the suggested baking time, then check back every 5 minutes; brownies can go from oozy to overcooked surprisingly quickly. Don't be afraid of taking brownies out of the oven when there's still a little movement in the middle. They firm up more as they cool.

why are my brownies taking so long?
Be patient, and resist the urge to whack up the temperature. Give the brownies a little more time, checking back every 5 minutes. If they're looking too browned on top, cover the tin with foil. On those occasions when you take brownies or blondies out of the oven, only to later realise they're completely undercooked (we've all done it), let the tin cool, then pop it in the fridge to help them set a bit more.

why does my batter look split?
Brownies involve mixing ingredients at different temperatures together, so if anything is too hot or cold, it can cause the mixture to seize or split. If your brownie batter looks oily or greasy, it's probable the chocolate and butter mixture has overheated. To avoid this, make sure you melt the chocolate and butter very gently, on as low a heat as possible. To safeguard against overheating even more, you can also melt the butter and chocolate in a heatproof bowl over a saucepan of barely-simmering water, rather than directly in the pan.

When a recipe calls for you to let the butter and chocolate mixture cool before adding the eggs and other ingredients, don't be tempted to skip this step (unless you like scrambled egg brownies). If you do find your batter has curdled, try mixing in a tablespoon or 2 of milk; it often brings everything back together.

how can I stop brownies going stale?

Eat them quicker, make more friends – or keep them in the fridge, especially if they contain wet ingredients like fresh fruit. Brownies and blondies also freeze superbly. Some people swear by putting a few slices of white bread into the tin and leaving overnight; the brownies draw moisture from the bread and will be softer and tastier the next day.

do I have to use 70% dark choc?

This is dangerous ground, you brownie maverick. I recommend dark chocolate with at least 70% cocoa solids because it provides a robust, chocolatey flavour. Using a lower percentage not only risks dampening the chocolatiness of your brownies, but it might also upset the success of the recipe. Try not to drop below 50% if you can help it. If you find dark chocolate too bitter, choose a recipe which uses a mix of dark and milk chocolate, such as the 'Tea and sympathy' brownies on page 32.

how can I make them more indulgent?

Gooier brownies tend to use less flour, so the first thing you can do is add a little less of the white stuff. They're also higher in sugar and butter, though these proportions are harder to tweak without risking the success of the recipe. One trick is to add an extra egg yolk; it won't affect the science of the recipe too much, but will make the brownies richer.

can I use a different tin size?

These recipes will probably work in a slightly smaller or bigger tin – an 18cm instead of a 20cm, for example – but the brownies will cook a little faster or slower, so be prepared to keep a careful eye on them. If you want to bake brownies in a significantly different-sized tin, you'll need to do some basic maths. The 20cm square tin I recommend has an area of 400 square centimetres; work out the area of the tin you want to use, and scale the ingredient quantities up or down accordingly. If you wanted to use a 25cm tin, for example, that would mean an area of 632 square centimetres, so you'd need to increase my ingredient quantities by a little more than a third. If all this fills you with a panic you haven't felt since secondary school geometry, you can find many useful guides to adjusting tin sizes online. And lots of cheap 20cm tins.

brownies
(sort of)

cracked brownie cookies

chewy, gooey, oooh-y

The lovechild of a brownie and a cookie. Inspired by a recipe by baking expert Edd Kimber, they have a chewy crust and a squidgy middle. You can also eat them sandwiched around ice cream. They are best eaten within a day or two (if they last that long).

Makes 12

200g dark chocolate
(around 70% cocoa solids),
roughly broken into pieces
100g unsalted butter,
chopped into rough cubes
50g dark muscovado sugar
150g caster sugar
2 large eggs
170g plain flour
½ teaspoon baking powder
½ teaspoon bicarbonate
of soda
¼ teaspoon salt
100g milk chocolate, finely
chopped into chunks
1 tablespoon granulated
sugar

1   Preheat the oven to 180°C/160°C Fan/Gas Mark 4. Line your 2 biggest baking trays with baking parchment.

2   Put the dark chocolate and the butter in a saucepan over a low heat and melt together, stirring regularly. Take off the heat and scrape into a bowl to cool for 5–10 minutes.

3   Put the dark muscovado sugar and caster sugar in a large clean bowl. Crack in the eggs. Beat with a handheld electric whisk for around 4 minutes, until pale and fluffy. Slowly pour the melted chocolate and butter into the bowl and fold in gently. Sift over the flour, baking powder, bicarbonate of soda and salt, and mix until just combined. Stir in the milk chocolate chunks. This will be an unusually wet cookie mixture – definitely not something you can handle with your hands!

4   You will now need to move quite quickly, before the mixture stiffens up. Use a tablespoon or dessert spoon to take out a heaped scoop of the mixture, and place on the lined baking tray (I usually use another spoon to help release the scoop onto the tray). Repeat with the rest of the mixture. You should be able to get around 12 cookies altogether, 6 on each tray; just make sure to leave plenty of room between the cookies, as they spread.

5   Sprinkle each cookie with a little granulated sugar and bake for 12–14 minutes. The tray on the lower shelf usually cooks a little slower, so may benefit from another minute or so once the top tray has been removed. Leave to cool for at least 15 minutes on the trays – they will be very soft – and then transfer to a rack to finish cooling.

brownie tiramisu trifle
coffee, marsala, custard

Two classic desserts, tiramisu and trifle, team up like Batman and Superman in one big, joyful, dig-in bowl.* I use good-quality ready-made custard in this because I'm incurably lazy, but homemade is even better if you have time. Marsala is a fortified wine from Sicily, whose sweetness counteracts the bitterness of the coffee. Serve the rest of the bottle alongside.

serves 6–8

500ml ready-made chilled custard
150g dark chocolate, chopped into rough chunks
pinch of salt
400–500g 'Ultimate fudgy brownies' (see page 20) or your other favourite brownie, cut into roughly 3cm chunks (the exact amount will depend on the size of your trifle bowl)
200ml strong, hot coffee
80–100ml sweet marsala
400ml double cream
40g caster sugar
250g mascarpone

1 Put the custard and the chocolate in a saucepan with the salt. Gently heat, stirring, until the chocolate has melted. Leave to one side to cool.

2 Put a few brownie chunks aside for later. Mix the coffee and 40ml of the marsala in a large shallow bowl. Dip the remaining brownie chunks one at a time into the mixture, turning them so they are well soaked, but moving quickly enough that they don't get soggy. Pile the chunks at the bottom of a trifle bowl, then top with the cooled chocolate custard, spreading so it completely covers the brownies. Cover and chill in the fridge for a few hours or overnight.

3 Shortly before you're ready to serve, put the double cream and sugar in a large bowl. Whip until soft peaks are just forming (be careful not to overwhip), then add the mascarpone and 40ml of the marsala. Gently whisk together until you have a smooth, creamy mixture; if it feels heavy and stiff, rather than pillowy-soft, mix in another 20ml of marsala. Pile on top of the custard. Crumble over the reserved brownie chunks and serve.

* My partner, reading this over my shoulder, points out that Batman is rarely joyful – but he might be if he tried a brownie tiramisu trifle.

eton mess blondie sundae

ice cream, meringue, strawberries

I'm always a bit thrilled by the prospect of an ice cream sundae. I think it's because they remind me of being a child, when I'd eye up these colourful, towering glasses through the window of seaside ice cream parlours; they looked so fantastical, as if they'd been scooped from the pages of a picture book. But it's also because made well, sundaes are delicious; a riotous, retro tumble of different flavours and textures that are more than the sum of their parts.

This sundae is a good way to use up the last blondies in the tin, and is easily adapted – try brownies and blueberries instead of blondies and strawberries, for example. A turret of what we British rather unappetisingly call 'squirty cream' is not necessary, but will make you smile – which is what sundaes are all about.

serves 2

200g strawberries
1 tablespoon caster sugar
½ teaspoon vanilla paste
    or extract
2 meringue nests
1–2 'Gentlemen prefer
    blondies' (see page 26)
    or your other favourite
    blondies
50g white chocolate
    (optional)
2 scoops of vanilla ice cream
2 scoops of strawberry
    ice cream
'squirty' cream (optional)

1   Roughly chop 150g of the strawberries and transfer to a small saucepan along with the caster sugar and 1 tablespoon of water. Cook over a low heat, stirring occasionally, for about 10 minutes until the strawberries have mostly collapsed into a jammy sauce. Stir in the vanilla extract and leave to cool and thicken.

2   Break the meringue nests into pieces and roughly chop the blondies into bite-size chunks. Slice the remaining strawberries in half and chop the white chocolate into small chunks, if using.

3   Assemble your sundaes – you can use individual glasses, or pile everything into a bowl to share. Layer up the ice cream scoops with the blondie bites, pieces of meringue, strawberry slices, chocolate chunks, if using, and most of the strawberry sauce. Add some squirty cream, if you like, then finish with a final drizzle of the sauce and a few slices of strawberry.

salted honey brownie truffles

chocolate, honey, sea salt

Homemade truffles look impressive but are secretly very easy. These are rich and creamy, speckled with dainty crumbs of brownie.

Serve to guests after dinner, with the pleased-yet-tired expression of someone who really made an effort.

makes 35–40

200g dark chocolate
(around 70% cocoa solids),
finely chopped
200ml double cream
6 tablespoons runny honey
30g unsalted butter,
chopped into rough cubes
200g 'Ultimate fudgy
brownies' (see page 20)
or your other favourite
brownies, crumbled with
your hands into fine
crumbs
1 teaspoon flaky sea salt,
plus extra to serve
80g cocoa powder

1 Put the chocolate in a bowl. In a saucepan over a low heat, gently heat the cream, honey and butter, stirring occasionally, until the butter is melted and the cream is steaming (but before it has started to simmer). Take off the heat and pour over the chocolate. Stir together until the chocolate is melted and you have a smooth mixture. Stir in the brownie crumbs and the salt. Let the mix cool, then cover and chill in the fridge for 3–4 hours, until firm.

2 To shape the truffles, dip a teaspoon into a mug of just-boiled water, then use it to scoop out a little mixture and form into small balls about the size of a walnut (you can also use a melon baller, if you have one). You may wish to gently roll each ball in your hands to make the truffles more even; dusting your hands with cocoa powder will stop them sticking so much, though it will still be a messy job.

3 Put the cocoa powder onto a plate and roll each truffle in it until evenly covered. Place the truffles onto a lined baking tray or plate, spaced slightly apart, and chill in the fridge for at least an hour. These will keep in a container in the fridge for 2 weeks, and can also be frozen. Serve sprinkled with extra sea salt, if liked.

figgy blondie pie
chocolate pastry, figs, tahini

Tahini, figs and chocolate are a luscious trio. I first made this one sunny Saturday when friends were coming over. We ate it after lunch in the garden, with a scoop of ice cream and a drizzle of honey, and strong black coffee on the side.

serves 12

for the pastry
200g plain flour
30g cocoa powder
pinch of salt
150g cold unsalted butter,
    chopped into small cubes
70g icing sugar
2 large egg yolks

for the filling
120g unsalted butter
3 figs
240g light brown soft sugar
2 large eggs, lightly beaten
150g plain flour
¼ teaspoon baking powder
80g tahini
100g white chocolate,
    chopped into small chunks

1   To make the pastry, put the flour, cocoa powder, salt and butter in a food processor and whizz until you have a mixture that resembles breadcrumbs. Add the icing sugar and egg yolks and whizz again, until the mixture clumps together and pulls away from the sides of the bowl. You can add a small splash of water if the pastry isn't coming together, but you shouldn't need to. (Alternatively, you can rub the dry ingredients and butter together with your fingertips in a large bowl, then mix in the egg.) Shape into a rough disc, then wrap in clingfilm and chill for at least 1 hour.

2   Preheat the oven to 190°C/170°C Fan/Gas Mark 5. Roll out the pastry on a well-floured surface to a thickness of about 4mm. Press firmly into a 24cm tart tin, then trim away any overhanging edges. Prick the bottom with a fork, line with baking parchment and fill with baking beans or rice. Bake for 20 minutes, then remove the paper and beans and bake for another 8–10 minutes. Take out of the oven, leaving the oven on, and set aside while you make the filling.

3   Melt the butter in a saucepan over a low heat. Take off the heat and leave to cool for 5 minutes. Slice each fig vertically into 5–6 thin slices.

4   Stir the sugar into the melted butter, then mix in the eggs. Sift in the flour and baking powder, then gently fold together until you have a smooth mix. Add the tahini and stir gently to mix in. Stir through the white chocolate chunks.

5 Spoon the mixture into the pastry case, and smooth out the top with a spatula or the back of the spoon. Arrange the fig slices over the top. Bake for 45–50 minutes, until set and golden on top; it should only have a very faint movement in the centre when you shake the tin. Be careful not to overbake. Let it cool completely, or until only just warm, before slicing.

banoffee brownie cake

bananas, caramel, cream

I have a soft spot for banoffee pie, that ludicrously OTT concoction of whipped cream, gooey toffee and bananas. Here, the flavours of banoffee pie are introduced to a brownie-style chocolate cake, with inevitably delicious results.

serves 12

for the cake

270g dark chocolate (around 70% cocoa solids), roughly broken into pieces
220g unsalted butter, chopped into rough cubes, plus extra for greasing
300g golden caster sugar
100g light brown soft sugar
4 large eggs, lightly beaten
160g plain flour
40g cocoa powder
1 teaspoon baking powder
½ teaspoon salt

for the filling

300ml double cream
100g caramel sauce (I use Carnation caramel)

to decorate

3 bananas
60g light brown soft sugar
40g butter
4–6 tablespoons caramel sauce

1 Preheat the oven to 180°C/160°C Fan/Gas Mark 4. Grease and line 2 x 20cm cake tins with baking parchment.

2 Melt the chocolate and butter in a large saucepan over a low heat, stirring regularly, until smooth and glossy. Stir in both sugars and take off the heat. Let it cool for around 5 minutes.

3 Add the eggs and beat well to combine. Sift in the flour, cocoa powder, baking powder and salt, and gently fold in to create a smooth batter. Divide the batter between the tins and transfer to the oven, ideally on the same shelf. Bake for 25–30 minutes; the cakes should be set on top, not wobbling at all, though a skewer inserted into the cakes will still come out with some crumbs. Leave to cool in the tins for 10 minutes, then turn out onto a wire rack to cool completely.

4 To make the filling, beat the double cream with an electric or balloon whisk until you have soft peaks. Gently stir through the caramel, to create a ripple effect.

5 Cut 2 of the bananas into 5mm slices. Put the sugar and butter in a large frying pan over a medium heat, stirring until melted together. As soon as the mixture starts to bubble, add the slices of banana and turn to coat. Cook for 2–3 minutes, stirring occasionally, until the bananas are nicely sticky and golden. (Don't cook the bananas too much longer as they can turn mushy.) Scoop out the slices with a slotted spoon, making sure you leave behind lots of the lovely sauce, and put on a plate to cool. Slice the

remaining banana in half lengthways and quickly add to the pan. Cook for few minutes on one side until golden, then flip over to cook the other side. Transfer to a plate to cool completely.

6 To assemble, put one of the cakes on a cake stand or plate, and spoon over a generous layer of the caramel sauce. Top with half the cream mixture, spreading out across the cake, then top with the caramelised sliced bananas. Put the other cake on top. Top with the rest of the cream and arrange the banana halves on top. Drizzle over any remaining caramel sauce to finish (if it's too thick to drizzle, heat in the microwave in short bursts until a little looser). Serve with plenty of napkins.

malted brownie pots
melting middles, malted milk

I have a committed relationship with gooey-centred desserts. It is impossible for me to not order one if it's on the menu at a restaurant, even if the taxi is already waiting outside. Sinking a spoon through the firm top to reveal the molten secret beneath is a great sensory pleasure, even better than the crunch of a crisp sandwich, or that popping noise when you open a new jar of jam.

These individual pots are flavoured with malt, in the form of both drinking powder and crushed Malteser chocolates; it goes very well with chocolate.

serves 6

120g Maltesers
*150g unsalted butter,
    chopped into rough cubes,
    plus extra for greasing*
*150g dark chocolate (around
    70% cocoa solids), roughly
    broken into pieces*
*2 large eggs and 1 large
    egg yolk*
100g caster sugar
100g light brown soft sugar
40g plain flour, sifted
*40g malted milk drink
    powder, such as Horlicks*
pinch of salt

1 Lightly grease 6 heatproof ramekins, between 120ml and 150ml in size, with a little butter. Preheat the oven to 180°C/160°C Fan/Gas Mark 4. Put the Maltesers in a plastic bag and gently crush with the end of a rolling pin, so you have some large and some smaller chunks.

2 Put the butter and chocolate in a small saucepan over a low heat and melt together, stirring occasionally. Take off the heat and leave to cool for 10 minutes.

3 Put the eggs and sugars in a large bowl and beat, using an electric mixer, for 5–8 minutes, until thick and pale. Little by little, pour the melted chocolate into the bowl, and gently fold in until combined.

4 Sift the flour and malted milk powder into the bowl, add a pinch of salt, and gently fold together.

5 Spoon the mixture into ramekins, leaving about a third in the bowl. Scatter over a few chunks of Maltesers, then spoon over the rest of the mix to cover. Don't fill the ramekin more than two-thirds, as the puddings will rise in the oven. Sprinkle the remaining Maltesers over the top. Bake for around 18–20 minutes until set on top, but still gooey in the middle. Serve immediately, before they collapse under their chocolatey weight.

plum and brownie cobbler

stone fruit, star anise

There is a family of comforting American desserts featuring baked fruit under a buttery topping, a little like the British crumble, but with better names, like 'grunt' and 'slump' and 'buckle'. As soon as the weather turns cold, I invite them into my kitchen. Here, I've given a classic plum cobbler a brownie-inspired makeover by adding chocolate to its scone-like topping. The star anise adds a tingle of spice.

Plums vary in sweetness, so try one before baking. If they're very sweet, you may want to use a little less sugar when roasting.

serves 6

800g plums, stoned and cut
    into chunky wedges
100g demerara sugar
1 tablespoon cornflour
juice of ½ small orange
3 star anise

for the cobbler topping

100g unsalted butter, chilled
    and chopped into rough
    cubes
50g dark brown sugar
50g demerara sugar, plus
    1–2 tablespoons for the
    topping
200g self-raising flour
50g cocoa powder
large pinch of salt
150g natural yoghurt
1 large egg yolk
100g milk chocolate,
    chopped into small chunks

1   Preheat the oven to 200°C/180°C Fan/Gas Mark 6.

2   Put the plums, sugar, cornflour, orange juice and star anise in a medium-sized baking dish and toss together. Roast for 15 minutes while you make the topping.

3   Put the butter, sugars, flour and cocoa powder in a large bowl with a large pinch of salt and rub together with your fingertips until you have a mixture that resembles breadcrumbs (alternatively, you can pulse together in a food mixer).

4   Mix the yoghurt and egg yolk together in a separate bowl, then add to the breadcrumb mixture. Use a spoon to start bringing it together into a sticky but firm dough, using your hands when it gets more difficult. Be gentle, as you don't want to overwork the dough and make it tough. Mix in the chocolate chips.

5   Divide the dough into rough balls, a little larger than golf balls, and flatten slightly with your hands. Take the baking dish out of the oven and arrange the dough balls over the plums, leaving small gaps between them so you can still see the fruit. Scatter over the extra demerara sugar. Bake for 30–35 minutes, until the topping is just set. I like this with cream or vanilla ice cream.

---

brownies (sort of)

gingerbread brownie muffins
dates, spices, ginger

I first made these for a picnic. I love picnics, though the anticipation of them (planning the food, filling the basket, picking out my waftiest dress) is often better than the reality (wasps with an eye on my sandwiches, rain, strange dogs with an eye on my sandwiches, rain). These muffins, however, will not disappoint. They're robust enough to survive being crushed under cans of G&T, and have a strong kick of spice to warm you up when the showers arrive.

makes 12

100g dark chocolate (around 70% cocoa solids), roughly broken into pieces
70g unsalted butter, chopped into rough cubes
150g natural yoghurt
50ml whole milk
70g dark muscovado sugar
2 large eggs, lightly beaten
150g plain flour
50g cocoa powder
1 tablespoon baking powder
1 teaspoon ground ginger
1 teaspoon ground cinnamon
¼ teaspoon ground cloves
pinch of salt
100g dates, pitted and finely chopped
80g crystallised ginger, finely chopped

1 Preheat the oven to 200°C/180°C Fan/Gas Mark 6 and line a 12-hole muffin tin with paper cases.

2 Put the chocolate and butter in a large saucepan over a low heat and gently melt together, stirring occasionally. Take off the heat and leave to cool for 5 minutes or so.

3 Add the yoghurt, milk, sugar and eggs and whisk together.

4 Sift the flour and cocoa powder into a separate bowl, then add the baking powder, spices and a pinch of salt, and stir to combine. Tip into the wet ingredients, along with the dates and crystallised ginger pieces, and gently combine, being careful not to over-mix.

5 Divide the mixture between the muffin cases. Bake for 20–25 minutes until risen and a skewer comes out clean. Remove from the tin and transfer to a wire rack to cool.

brownie mince pies

brown sugar pastry, cinnamon sugar

A velvety mince pie, served under a snow drift of spiced icing sugar. These are perfect for all your Christmas needs; offer them to friends who drop round with gifts, pop one in your pocket for the walk to the carol service and feed leftover pastry to the birds, like a festive Mary Poppins. Brown sugar pastry has a wonderful caramel flavour but is soft and fragile; don't be tempted to skip the chilling stage, and handle as delicately as a child who didn't get the Christmas present they asked for.

makes 12

for the brown sugar pastry
220g plain flour
140g cold unsalted butter, cubed
40g light brown soft sugar
½ teaspoon mixed spice or cinnamon
pinch of salt
1 large egg
1 teaspoon vanilla paste or extract

for the filling
60g unsalted butter, chopped into rough cubes
80g dark chocolate (around 70% cocoa solids), roughly broken into pieces
90g caster sugar
1 large egg, lightly beaten
40g plain flour
¼ teaspoon salt
150g mincemeat

1   To make the pastry, put the flour, butter, sugar, mixed spice or cinnamon and a generous pinch of salt in a food processor and whizz until the mixture resembles breadcrumbs. Add the egg and vanilla extract and whizz briefly until the pastry comes together into a dough. (Alternatively, you can rub the dry ingredients and butter together with your fingertips in a large bowl, then mix in the egg and vanilla extract.) Shape into a rough disc, then wrap in clingfilm and chill for at least 1 hour.

2   Preheat the oven to 180°C/160°C Fan/Gas Mark 4. Roll out the pastry on a very well-floured surface until it's about 3mm in thickness. This is quite a fragile pastry, so be generous with the flour, and don't be tempted to roll it any thinner or it's likely to break. Use an 8-inch straight-sided cookie cutter to stamp out 12 rounds, and use these to line a 12-hole muffin tin. You may need to re-roll the pastry scraps to make all 12 cases. Prick the bases with a fork, and put the tin in the fridge to chill for 15–20 minutes.

3   While the pastry is chilling, start the filling. Put the butter and chocolate in a heatproof bowl set over a saucepan of just-simmering water saucepan, and melt together, stirring occasionally. Take off the heat, stir in the sugar and leave for 5 minutes or so to cool slightly.

for the cinnamon sugar
1 tablespoon icing sugar
1 teaspoon cinnamon

4 Beat in the egg, then sift in the flour and salt, and gently fold in to make a smooth mixture. Add the mincemeat and fold in. Fill each pastry case with a heaped dessertspoonful of the mixture. Bake for 20–25 minutes, until the pastry is golden. Leave to cool for 10 minutes or so in the tin, then carefully transfer to a wire rack to finish cooling. To serve, mix the icing sugar with the cinnamon, and sift over the mince pies.

brownie mudslide

irish cream, coffee, chocolate

There is a time and place for classy, classic cocktails like a Manhattan or Negroni, but occasionally, I'm in the mood for something sweet and silly, more akin to a dessert than a drink, with a naff name – and in this case, a brownie-studded chocolate rim. Cheers.

serves 2

40–50g brownie of your choice (a cakey or slightly stale brownie works best)
60g dark or milk chocolate
60ml coffee-flavoured liqueur
60ml Irish cream, such as Baileys
60ml vodka
80ml double cream

1 Use your hands to break the brownie into fine crumbs over a plate. Roughly chop 40g of the chocolate, put it in a shallow bowl and heat in the microwave in 10-second bursts, stirring in-between, until smooth and melted. Dip the rim of 2 short, tumbler-style glasses in the melted chocolate, then dip them into the brownie crumbs until well coated. Put in the fridge briefly to firm up.

2 Put the coffee liquor, Irish cream, vodka and double cream in a cocktail shaker or jam jar with ice. Seal and shake vigorously until cold and well mixed. Pour into the glasses, being careful not to disturb the rim. Grate over the remaining chocolate. You can also garnish this with a piece of brownie on a cocktail stick, for an added chocolate hit.

brownie pancakes
cherries, chocolate, amaretto

Breakfast is one of the great joys of the weekend. Whether it's pancakes or a fry-up, starting the day with a proper, leisurely meal is good for the soul.* These American-style pancakes, dimpled with cherries and dolloped with a rich chocolate sauce, are one of my favourite weekend treats. They also make an easy and delicious dessert. You can leave out the amaretto if you're not quite ready for it on a Saturday morning.

serves 4 (about 12 pancakes)

for the pancakes
300g fresh cherries
170g plain flour
30g cocoa powder
3 tablespoons light brown soft sugar
2 teaspoon baking powder
¼ teaspoon salt
40g unsalted butter, melted, plus extra for cooking
2 large eggs
240ml whole milk

for the chocolate amaretto sauce
150ml double cream
2 tablespoons golden syrup
100g dark chocolate, roughly chopped
3–4 tablespoons amaretto

1   Destone the cherries. This is easy to do by putting them in a plastic bag, then using a rolling pin to break them open, before popping out the stones. Roughly chop 200g, and slice the remaining 100g in half and put to one side.

2   Sift the flour, cocoa powder, sugar, baking powder and salt into a large bowl and stir together. Create a well in the centre with a spoon, then add the melted butter, eggs and milk. Whisk together to make a thick batter, then stir in the 200g of roughly-chopped cherries.

3   Heat a knob of butter in a large non-stick frying pan over a medium heat. When the butter starts to bubble, dollop in a generous spoonful of the batter – I usually find it easiest to use a ladle, filling it just under half-full for each pancake. Aim for your pancakes to be around 8cm wide; you should be able to cook 2 or 3 at a time, depending on the size of your pan.

4   Cook the pancakes until bubbles start to appear on the surface (usually about 2 minutes), then flip the pancakes over and cook for a minute or so more. Repeat with the remaining batter. Keep cooked pancakes warm in a low oven, or on a plate set over of a bowl of just-boiled water, loosely covered with a tea towel.

5 To make the chocolate sauce, put the double cream and golden syrup in a medium saucepan over a low heat. Heat gently until it starts to bubble at the edges, then take off the heat and add the chocolate. Let it sit for 1–2 minutes, then gently stir, until the chocolate has melted and you have a smooth, glossy sauce. Stir in 3 tablespoons of the amaretto, then taste and add a little more if you like. Serve the pancakes with the sauce, and the reserved halved cherries.

* It's certainly a more calming experience than throwing pieces of toast at your children's faces as you chase them out the door.

the brownie friendship circle

Make brownies even better by serving them alongside one of these delicious ingredients, all of which have an affinity with chocolate.

caramel

A puddle of caramel sauce transforms a brownie instantly from casual afternoon snack to come-hither dinner party dessert. Though salted caramel arguably pours its sticky rivulets into too many recipes nowadays (I'm not convinced anybody needs salted caramel crisps), it does work magnificently with brownies. To make a quick version, simply melt 180g light brown soft sugar, 300ml double cream and 50g butter together in a saucepan over a low heat, and bubble for a few minutes until thick. Add salt to taste, and flood your brownies, biblically.

coffee

Coffee and chocolate have a lot in common; they're both made from bitter beans that undergo an intensive process before they reach your kitchen, and contain similar dark, earthy and fruity flavour notes. A cup of coffee on the side of a brownie is a restorative pleasure, each bringing out the flavours of the other. Adding a little coffee to a brownie mixture can also intensify the bake's chocolatiness, without making them taste of coffee. Try 'I don't have any chocolate brownies', page 65, or add ½ teaspoon of espresso powder to your favourite recipe.

crème fraîche

Ice cream or cream are traditional accompaniments to chocolate desserts, but crème fraîche is the grown-up choice; its tanginess offsets the indulgent sweetness of brownies.

vanilla

Anyone who has ever enjoyed a scoop of chocolate ice cream next to a scoop of vanilla knows that these two ingredients sing very sweetly and politely together, neither overwhelming each other. Niki Segnit writes in her book, *The Flavour Thesaurus*, that their intertwinement in our minds may be due to the fact that many chocolate makers include vanilla in their bars. Cold vanilla-speckled custard is delicious with brownies; I also like whipped cream, mixed with 1 teaspoon of vanilla bean paste.

berries

Brownies topped with summer berries were the *de rigueur* pud of the 1990s gastropub and it's a classic combination for a reason. The fresh, tangy fruit balances the brownies' richness, and it looks pretty, too. Sharper berries, like raspberries and blackberries, work better than the more straightforward (dare I say flatter?) sweetness of strawberries.

nuts

Cocoa beans often develop nutty flavour notes as part of the chocolate-making process, so it's no surprise nuts and brownies are contented bedfellows. The harmony is about more than just flavour; a good sweet treat always contains a balance of different textures, and a mouthful of crunchy nuts is perfect alongside brownies' soft squidginess. You can of course bake brownies with nuts inside, but I usually prefer a plain chocolate brownie served with a scoop of ice cream, and a sprinkling of nuts on top. Most nuts work, though almonds, hazelnuts and walnuts are particularly good. Toast your nuts to intensify their flavour, or cook them with a little butter and sugar so they become sticky and caramelised. Nut brittle – a mosaic of nuts, suspended in glass-like shards of crunchy sugar – always looks beautiful.

port

Choosing an alcohol that pairs well with brownies is a little like finding a date for your loudest, bolshiest friend; you need something (or someone) pretty powerful to match their intensity. A sticky fortified wine like port will stand up to a brownie admirably. Another, more interesting option, is the French dessert wine Banyuls; a little like port, but livelier and fruitier, it brings a zip of freshness and acidity.

index

about the author

Leah Hyslop is a food writer and editor. She worked at *The Telegraph* and then *Sainsbury's Magazine* before becoming Deputy Editor at *Waitrose and Partners Food* magazine.

Her first book, *Made in London*, was published in 2018. Leah now lives just outside of the city, and is still finding brownie crumbs all over the house.

thank yous

A book is always a team effort. Thanks to Lauren and Vicki, for making all those squares of brown look so different and delicious. Thank you to my agent Juliet, and the wonderful team at Absolute – Jon, Meg, Emily and Anika. I'm very proud to be part of the Bloomsbury family … and deeply sorry that due to the pandemic, I didn't get to feed you all more brownies. And not forgetting Craig and Ed the cat, for keeping me sane – just about.

credits

publisher
Jon Croft

commissioning editor
Meg Boas

senior editor
Emily North

art director & designer
Anika Schulze

photographer
Lauren Mclean

stylist
Vicki Smallwood

home economist
Adam O'Shepherd

proofreader
Kate Wanwimolruk

indexer
Zoe Ross